The travels of Major C. Bolin while he was a fugitive, and after his capture by deputy-sheriff "Whisky" Jackson, are indicated by the red lines on this map.

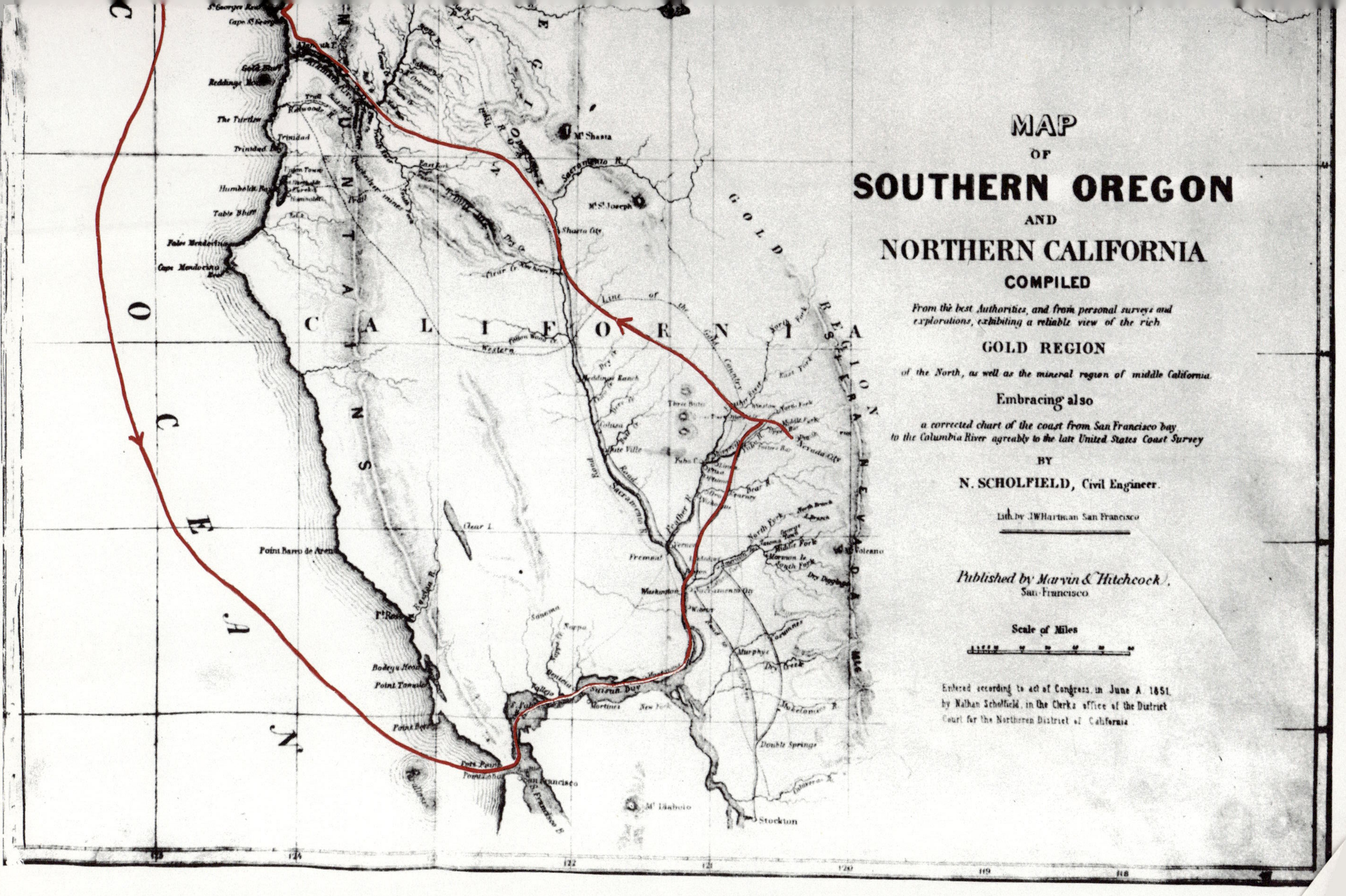
MAP
OF
SOUTHERN OREGON
AND
NORTHERN CALIFORNIA
COMPILED
From the best Authorities, and from personal surveys and explorations, exhibiting a reliable view of the rich
GOLD REGION
of the North, as well as the mineral region of middle California
Embracing also
a corrected chart of the coast from San Francisco bay to the Columbia River agreably to the late United States Coast Survey
BY
N. SCHOLFIELD, Civil Engineer.
Lith. by J.W.Hartman San Francisco
Published by Marvin & Hitchcock,
San-Francisco
Scale of Miles
Entered according to act of Congress, in June A. 1851, by Nathan Scholfield, in the Clerks office of the District Court for the Northern District of California
GOLD REGION
SIERRA NEVADA
CALIFORNIA
MOUNTAINS
OCEAN
Mt. Shasta
Mt. St. Joseph
Shasta City
Sacramento R.
Feather R.
Suisun Bay
San Francisco
San Francisco B.
Mt. Diablo
Stockton
Sacramento City
Nevada City
Three Buttes
Clear L.
Point Barro de Arena
Bodega Head
Point Tamales
Point Reyes
Humboldt Bay
Table Bluff
Trinidad
Cape Mendocino
False Mendocino
Sonoma
Napa
Benicia
Vallejo
Martinez
New York
Fremont
Washington
Murphys
Double Springs
Volcano
Dry Diggings
Redding's Ranch
Colusa
Line of the Gold Country
Western
Road
124
122
121
120
119
118

Life and Adventures
OF
MAJOR C. BOLIN

STOVES & TINWARE

NARRATIVE

OF THE

Life and Adventures

OF

MAJOR C. BOLIN,

ALIAS

DAVID BUTLER,

AS RELATED BY HIMSELF
TO A. A. SARGENT

YE GALLEON PRESS
FAIRFIELD, WASHINGTON

Library of Congress Cataloging-in-Publication Data

Bolin, Major C., 1830-1858.
Narrative of the life and adventures of Major C. Bolin, alias David Butler / as related by himself to A.A. Sargent.
p. cm.
Originally published: Palo Alto, Ca. : L. Osborne, 1966.
Includes bibliographical references (p.) and index.
ISBN 0-87770-580-1 (hard case). -- ISBN 0-87770-581-X (paper)
1. Bolin, Major C., 1830-1858. 2. California--History--1850-1950. 3. California--Gold discoveries. 4. Violence--California--History--19th century. 5. Gamblers--California--Biography. 6. Murderers--California--Biography. 7. Oregon-- History--To 1859. 8. Frontier and pioneer life--California.
I. Sargent, A.A. (Aaron Augustus), 1827-1887.
F864.B65 1996
979.4'092--dc20

96-4603
CIP

Previously printed by

Lewis Osborne : Palo Alto, 1966

INTRODUCTION

Crime and punishment have fascinated mankind since Cain slew Abel. Nowhere has this been more evident than in the literature of the American West. Violence was so long a way of life west of the Missouri River that those who eventually supplanted brute force with law and order often had to ape it, with vigilantism, in order to counteract it effectively.

The California Mother Lode, after the Gold Rush, remained a hothouse for crime and general lawlessness for many years. One of the great cases of that day and area was *The People vs. David Butler*. It is best known, perhaps, from the brief and garbled account given by Major William Downie in his book *Searching For Gold* in 1893. Just as Grizzly Adams was not the James Capen Adams he claimed to be, and just as Talbot H. Green was not the man he seemed to be, so David Butler was "someone else." The name was an alias adopted by an Ohio Argonaut in 1853 when he became a gambler in the California mining camps. His real name was Major C. Bolin, the Major being his given name and not a military title.

Bolin epitomized the wayward young emigrants of whom the San Francisco *Daily Alta California* complained more than a century ago, the gold-seekers who forgot all familial admonitions and strayed further and further from the straight and narrow trail once they were out West. Cried the *Alta:* "They sink lower and lower until they become thieves, robbers, and desperadoes." Bolin was neither thief nor robber and, if a desperado technically, he was the sort of desperate man whose manhandling by fate excites the sympathy of the reader rather than his hostility.

But Bolin's sad and short career proves the validity of the Victorian cliché in regard to ruination following association with "bad company." With the hangman's noose around his neck, Bolin lectured an audience of almost 5,000 men and women: "My advice is to you all to shun bad company, ever be your own counsel, and never be led astray by the bad . . . I hope my fate will be a warning to all."

Major C. Bolin was a clergyman's son turned gambler and drunkard. He exemplified magnificently all of the victims of quick and easy money in El Dorado. But this prodigal blacksheep who was hanged by the neck until dead on February 26, 1858, at the ripe age of 27 years, proved himself to be anything but a weakling when he was on the run from the law. No reader can fail to be impressed by his courage.

The son of a Pickaway County, Ohio, farmer, Bolin was doubtless descended from kin of Anne Boleyn of unhappy fate. He migrated with his family to the prairies of Pike County, Illinois, in 1838, when he was only eight years old. Major's father was doubly a pillar of Illinois society, being not only a farmer but a preacher of the Campbellite persuasion in that pious county where revivalism, shouting and "the jerks" were all religiously *de riguer*. When a mugbook history of the county was published in 1880, it called attention to the fine and upstanding Bolin family not only by the usual laudatory page of text but with a portrait of Major's older brother, John O. Bolin. Nowhere in the biographical sketch of this proud and prosperous man of Milton, Illinois, is there the faintest mention of his brave, if ill-starred, brother. But this was only to be expected from a proper and godly family in the intolerant Victorian Midwest.

Bolin had become a gamblin' man, one of the men in whom, to use Bret Harte's words, "listless and grave indifference passed for good breeding." But where Harte's fictional gambler, John Oakhurst, was a professional who never fuzzed his dealer's brain with drink, the clergyman's son was only an amateur or an apprentice at cards, more accomplished as a drinker than as a monte or poker dealer. Pop-skull whiskey had more than a little to do with Bolin's plight; it blew up a two-bit tussle into a homicide which, after ruining his life, took it. Actually, it was the misfortune of both Oakhurst and Bolin to fall victim of what Harte called "a spasm of virtuous violence." These Puritanical reversions periodically convulsed Mother Lode towns, turning them into fair copies of Milton itself. Such a spasm made Oakhurst an outcast of Poker Flat; a similar convulsion drove Bolin into a desperate flight from Downieville which became more adventurous and exciting than even Ned Magowan's classic retreat from the San Francisco Vigilantes.

Aficionados of Western Americana will be struck with at least two features of Bolin's colorful story, besides the natural drama, suspense and pathos of the tragedy. First, they will notice the power of the narrative; Bolin was a gifted narrator. They will appreciate his natural superiority as a story-teller to Bret Harte, who drew directly on such cases as Bolin's for inspiration for his fiction but who flawed his stories in transforming them from reality to art by dosing them with melodrama and sentimentality until his pathos more nearly resembled bathos. Bolin's apologia rings as true as a Denver dollar. It is a story of the true West, not the romanticized West of Harte, Belasco and Puccini. Moreover, most readers will find Bolin convincing in his justification of

Moffat's death. He admitted shooting the man but resolutely insisted, until the trap was literally sprung, that the ball which killed Moffat in Craycroft's Saloon in Downieville, on the evening of September 27, 1855, came from the accidental discharge of the pistol in his hands during a struggle for the weapon. Persisted Bolin, "Whether or not he [Moffat] pulled it, or it was discharged by my excited movements, I am equally guiltless of any intention to take the life of Moffat."

Bolin, perhaps aided by the skill of his amanuensis and attorney, A. A. Sargent, made a very good case for himself in the *Narrative*, but it was already too late. Although Edward D. Baker, California's great orator and Oregon's Senator (until killed in the Civil War) moved that Bolin's indictment be set aside, and although Sargent, later a California Congressman and Senator, fought hard and long for his client, it was all over long before the trial. For, en route to San Francisco from Oregon, Bolin's guard, a Siskiyou County deputy named Jackson, either fell or was pushed overboard from the lumber schooner taking them to California. The man at the wheel was a witness, with Bolin, to the fact that Jackson fell; but *two* deaths in which he was involved totted up to a death warrant for the gambler.

It is impossible at this remove to state whether Bolin was guilty or not. His guilt was "proven" to the satisfaction of a Nevada City jury and he was executed. But no one can read his *Life and Adventures* without feeling that he was basically an honorable man, however dissipated he may have become in the Mines. There is conviction and the ring of truth on every page; nowhere does he whine. If Bolin deceives the reader, he is a master dissimulator. He admits to pistol-whipping Moffat but denies intent to kill. His character during his long flight from justice is anything but that of a dissolute weakling. On the very scaffold his bearing was impressive, a fact not at all lost on the editor of the *Nevada Democrat*—"Bolin stood on the scaffold a little over an hour and bore up to the very last with the most heroic firmness. There was nothing of bravado in his words or actions; he seemed to fully realize his situation and did not conceal his regret at leaving the world but exhibited no craven fear of death."

Unfortunately, Bolin was assumed to be guilty by public and press and, presumably, jurors long before he went to trial. Moffat was made out to be a loud-mouthed but harmless miner while "Butler" was damned as a gambler and no-good.

Major William Downie, the founder of Downieville, held no brief for Bolin, calling him a bully as well as a gambler, but he did not subscribe to the picture of Moffat as a mild fellow. He described him as "a man whose uncontrollable temper had, on many occasions, led him to the verge of disaster." The Major claimed that only a few days before the quarrel with Bolin, Moffat had moved the stakes of Philo Havens' claim, for which action the latter paid him with a punch betwixt the eyes and the prediction, "Moffat, you won't live another ten days!" Downie, who is (to say the least) not completely reliable as a reminiscer, introduced an explanation for Bolin's butting into a quarrel in which he had no part, a quarrel which exploded into a killing. Contradicting Bolin's flat statement ("I did not know Moffat at the time"), Downie claimed that the two men were rivals for the favors of an actress, Mrs. Marian Goodenow Robb, and that Bolin was ahead in the amatory race until Moffat hit upon the idea of salting his claim with a $400 shotgun charge of gold dust just before inviting the actress to try her hand at prospecting. Perhaps the contest ended in a draw; in any event, Marian departed from town with her traveling company, leaving behind both gambler and miner. But it was Downie's contention that the real cause of Bolin's poking his nose into Moffat's quarrel with the Mexican José María Núnêz, usually called Joe, was Marian, and Moffat's loud comment, as the gambler approached, "Here comes that scoundrel Bolin."

This explanation appears nowhere else, not in Bolin's account, nor in the comprehensive coverage of the trial by the *Weekly Sierra Citizen* of August 22, 1857 (nor even in the truly voluminous trial transcript and related documents kindly made available to this writer by Dr. William N. Davis, Historian of the California State Archives). As might be expected, the more than twenty witnesses called in Bolin's trial came up with approximately twenty versions of the actions and hot words of the Bolin-Moffat difficulty in Craycroft's Saloon on the night of September 27, 1855. But none of them connected the two men in any kind of amorous isosceles.

Bolin's account is of course a defense, but a study of the testimony of the many prosecution witnesses substantiates his version of the affair at least up to the point where his 8-inch Colt Navy revolver was, somehow, cocked and fired. The basic points are clear. Moffat hunted up a Mexican, Joe, in the saloon and in a loud and bullying tone, accused him of being the leader of a band of outlaws planning to rob his quartz mill near The Buttes. Joe protested his innocence, politely as befitted a "Mex" in 1855, but Bolin interceded in his behalf. Hot words were exchanged and Bolin, noting the fifty pounds he gave away to the burly Moffat, pulled his equalizer out of his waistband. Twice he swung his revolver as a club but, the third time, it went off and sent a ball into Moffat's side, just below the ribs. Two of his cronies rushed Bolin to the street and up the North Fork in a successful escape from a mob led by pistol-brandishing Judge Shaffer, who was crying "Catch him!"

After his recapture in Oregon, Bolin (still hiding his true identity under the alias David Butler to avoid embarrassing his family in Illinois) was locked up in the County Jail in Nevada City. He was indicted on April 8, 1857, by a Sierra County Grand Jury which his attorneys E. D. Baker, William M. Stewart, and A. A. Sargent claimed was illegally constituted. After a change of venue, he was tried before District Court Judge Niles Searls on August 10, 11 and 12, 1857, and found guilty of murder by a jury which needed only fifteen minutes and one ballot (unanimous) after hearing Judge Searls' instructions. Answering Sargent's argument that Moffat's offensive and insulting words drove Bolin to violence, the Justice charged, "No words are sufficient to reduce a homicide from murder to manslaughter." He added that, if Moffat had attempted no injury on Bolin, nor any provocation beyond words, "the Jury should find the prisoner guilty of murder."

On August 17, 1857, Judge Searls sentenced Bolin to death by hanging on Friday, October 9, but Sargent appealed to the State Supreme Court. The Justice who accepted the appeal was none other than David Terry who, himself, would die a violent death in an affray at Lathrop thirty-one years later. The Supreme Court upheld the District Court's decision and Bolin was re-sentenced to be hanged on December 11, 1857. Sargent and others contacted Governor J. Neely Johnson and, noting how short was the time between sentence and execution, the Governor granted a stay of execution until February 26, 1858. During that time Bolin hoped, vainly, to collect enough representations of his good character from Illinois, Oregon and California to induce the Governor to commute his death sentence. Johnson granted the stay, actually, to allow Bolin time to prepare fully for his fate.

Oregon knew Bolin not as David Butler but as Jack Hurley, although, curiously, nowhere in his *Narrative* does he mention this second go-by. The story of his stay in Oregon is an astounding saga of survival which ended when he staggered up to surrender to Major Joel Graham Trimble's company of soldiers en route to the Dalles from Walla Walla. It was a raw, wintry day and to Trimble the tattered fugitive looked as if he had been plucked. Bolin had had to cut off the tails of his long army overcoat in order to wrap up his bloody, frozen feet. He told the officer that he was so worn out from thirty-one days of fatigue, hunger and exposure that he could no longer evade the 300 Indians paid to hunt him down. (He did not mention that he had been shot, once in the back and once in the thigh.) The raw courage of the man was remarkable. He had fought off Indians attacking a friend, Jones, on the Chetco River and had dashed recklessly after the redskins as an army volunteer on the Umatilla. But his greatest exploit was to hide out in the winter wilderness for thirty-one days while whites and Indians alike searched relentlessly for him.

There is no doubt that Sargent's transcribing of Bolin's account, on February 4, 1858, and the subsequent publication of the work by N. P. Brown & Co. of Nevada City, was meant as a last, desperate move to win commutation of the sentence of death. But not even this hole-card could save the young gambler. Almost 5,000 people followed Bolin and his militia escort out to Lost Hill, where the gallows stood waiting. Many of these men and women must have secured copies of the *Narrative* to read, re-read, and pass on to others. Today, only one source can report a copy—the Henry E. Huntington Library, whose librarian, Mr. Robert Dougan, graciously put it at the service of the writer and his publisher in order to produce this first reprint edition of the document. As a part of Sargent's defense strategy in 1857–'58, the work was a failure. But as a documentation of the social history of the brutal frontier era, it will be of permanent value. More than a fascinating tale of escape and adventure, out-Harteing Bret at his best, it realistically depicts the dog-eat-dog life which has been romanticized into a kind of golden age of rugged individualism. Most of the best writers about the Gold Rush period, like Bayard Taylor or even Edwin Bryant, have been outsiders looking in. Bolin's gripping tale is an inside story. This is the way California and Oregon really were.

Although the *Narrative* failed to save Bolin's life, to anyone having a sense of history it is a cogent argument against the death penalty and, thus, may still be of some service to those who find themselves, one day, in Major Bolin's predicament.

RICHARD H. DILLON

San Francisco, May, 1966

THE FOLLOWING NARRATIVE was taken down by me at the dictation of Major C. Bolin, *alias* David Butler. I have preserved his style almost wholly, and his ideas exactly. I had been one of his counsel upon his trial, at Nevada (City), and after his sentence, knowing that many incidents of his life were peculiar, asked him to give me a statement of his history. He took time to consider of the matter; and on the 4th of February sent for me, and related his life as herein set down.

A. A. SARGENT

Nevada (City), February 12th, 1858.

Major C. Bolin

My real name is Major C. Bolin. I was born in Pickaway county Ohio, on the 7th of December, 1830, and am now twenty-seven years of age. My father, Charles Bolin, is a minister, of the Campbellite denomination, now living in Milton, Pike county, Illinois. By my parents I was strictly brought up, educated and well advised. I remember their conduct to me with respect and affection. My mother died in March, 1849. I have one brother and two sisters living in the neighborhood of my father, in Illinois. My business, up to my coming to California, most of the time, was attending to the affairs of a farm.

I left home on the 25th of March, 1850, for California, and arrived at Placerville, on the 3d of September. I, at once, went on to the American river, and engaged in mining near Coloma. I worked on the river until the rainy season set in, when I went to a place called Pilot Hill, and mined there. There I worked till about Christmas, when I was taken sick, and was sick until March, 1851, when I went to Cache Creek. At the Crossing of Cache Creek I hired with a man by the name of Cochran. I was still in poor health, and was kindly cared for by him. When able, I attended to his stock. In July, he told me he was willing to assist me, and advanced me three hundred dollars to buy the ranch claim of a squatter, adjoining Cochran's farm, on Cache Creek. I bought the claim, and worked about a month getting out rails, when I concluded to go to the mines again. I went to New York Bar, on the middle fork of the American river, and worked there about six weeks, when I returned to Cache Creek, and paid Cochran back his money. Soon after my return, a title to three leagues of land on Cache Creek, embracing my ranch, held by one Hardy, who had died some time before, was sold, and J. M.

Estelle, M. Harbin, ——— Parrish and ——— Tyler, finding it to be valid, bought it in. The citizens met together to bid off the right of the title, but let the persons above named bid it off on their promise to let the citizens have the land at Government prices. After these men had bid in the land they refused to let the citizens have their ranches of one hundred and sixty acres on the Creek, unless they would take as much more immediately back of them. I was unable to take the three hundred and twenty acres, and was compelled to sell out to one Hutton, who, at that time, kept a hotel on J street, Sacramento. I then went to Sacramento and stopped there a month at a hotel, my expenses soon using up most of my money. I then went again to Placerville, and engaged again in mining, and worked until March, 1852. I then went to the Cosumnes river, at a place called Grizzly Flat, and mined

In a miner's cabin, weighing gold.

PLACERVILLE (HANGTOWN).

there till June. I then returned to Placerville, and hired to a man by the name of John Phillips, sub-contractor for a large flume that was being built to convey water into that place. I worked for him two months. Up to this time I had earned an honest living, had not engaged in gambling, and had always tried to do right, so far as I knew. I had not indulged in liquor nor frequented any haunts of vice.

At Placerville I became acquainted with two gambling boys. When my two months' work was over they proposed to me to go South—said they were out of money, and asked me to pay their expenses. This I did till we came to Murphy's Camp. At that place one of them asked me to let him have my money to bet on the cards. I did so and he took it, but I did not bet any myself, at that time. He lost the money. After he lost it I told him that I would have to go to work, and that when he made a raise he could pay me back what he thought was right—that I was willing to stand a share of the loss. He told me that if he was in my place, he would not go to work, and that if I would go to one of the boys that I was acquainted with, I could borrow some money from him, and we could get even. I went and borrowed fifty dollars, and let him have it, and he lost it. I was then discouraged, and did not know what to do. He persuaded me that we would have better fortune soon—that he could get little stakes of gamblers. We went then to Angel's Camp; there he left me. At this place I met a young man that I had known at Placerville. He had some money, and proposed that we should go to prospecting and find diggings. We prospected about a month, and did not find much. I then proposed to him to go to Cache Creek with me. We came back to Jackson. I told him if he was willing I would try to win stage-

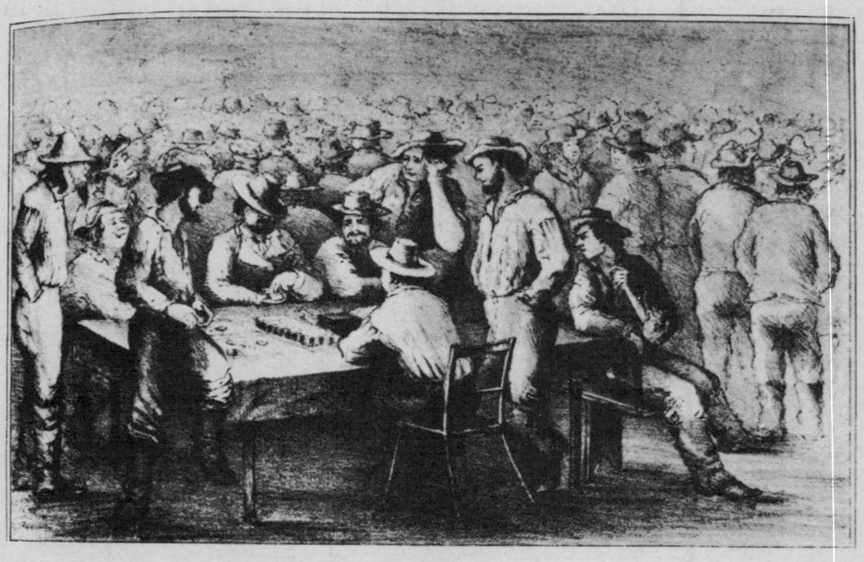

MINERS PLAYING MONTE.

A faro game in the Gold Country.

fare from there to Sacramento. He consented, and gave me some money, and I won the stage-fare at *monte*. We then started and went to Sacramento. I proposed to him there that I would try my luck again. He said he was willing, and gave me the money. I was lucky, and won some. We then went on to Cache Creek. I had some money coming to me there; got it and returned to Sacramento. I thought I would try my luck again, and lost all I had. I ought to have had a lesson by that time. My friend shared my fate. Upon this result we went again to Placerville, by way of Drytown. At the latter place I met a friend, who asked me if I was "broke;" I told him I was. He said he had money, and would loan me some if I wanted it. He loaned me some, and made a proposition, at the same time, to put in a stake with me, and try our luck against faro. I told him I had lost what money I had, and did not think I could beat anybody playing cards. He said it was not worth while to get downhearted; to come and take a drink, and to try, and perhaps we could get even. We went to play against faro, and I was very lucky. I won some four hundred dollars. In the meantime, I was drinking occasionally, to keep up the fashion with the other "sports." I don't recollect when I went to bed. I woke up without money. I hunted up my friend who had given me the money. He gave me more to bear my expenses, and I went to Placerville. At that place I related my adventures to a friend, and told him I wished to go to work. He said he would give me a chance in some diggings with himself. I worked about a month, and made nothing. This was in the spring of 1853. While I was mining, the proposition was made to go and pass an evening at Diamond Springs, by the boys in the claim. After we got in town, we went into a restaurant for supper, and while there a gambling man came in and said he was "broke," and wanted to put up a gold specimen breast-pin, at "freeze out" poker. One of my partners in the diggings proposed if I would play he would put in half. I went in and won the pin. I then played poker all night, still winning. I had too much money then to go to work again, and thought I would go to Placerville and try my luck against a faro game, and if I could have a little luck I would get even on all my gambling. I played in some luck two or three days, then lost all I had. Then a man made a proposition to me to go to Sacramento with him. He owed money, and had a team and went down for goods. After he got to Sacramento, he sold his team and told me he would bear my expenses if I would go to the Northern Mines with him. I told him I would do so. After we were on the boat, between Sacramento and Marysville, he told me he had sold his team, and owed money, and was leaving the debt unpaid; but when he "made a big raise" he would go back and pay it. He said his intention was to gamble; that he had gambled a great deal before he came to this country. He said if I would look out for him he would deal a game. We got to Marysville, and he bought a lot of *monte* cards. We left there next morning, and made our way to Rough and Ready, in Nevada county. I never had dealt any game of any kind, or assisted in dealing any, and did so at Rough and Ready for the first time. We won some two hundred dollars the first night, and then went to Grass Valley. This was late in the Fall of 1853. We soon lost all the money we both had, and then came to Nevada, where we stopped awhile. I then went to Forest City, having left my late companion at Nevada. At that place I went to work, getting out timber to build a house. I still gambled when I had money. Up to July, 1855, I made my home at Forest City, but would occasionally visit Downieville, Chipp's Flat and other places, to gamble. During that time I bought a claim and worked it some, but trusted to gambling, more than anything else, for a living—dealing a game at night. Some time in July 1855, I think, I went to Downieville, and remained there most of the time till September. I did not deal any game at Downieville, but played against the banks or at poker.

It was, I think, on the twenty-seventh day of September that the affray between myself and Robert Moffat happened, between 8 and 9 o'clock in the evening, at Craycroft's Saloon. I was in the back-room, playing cards, was considerably intoxicated, and had no hard feelings against any one. I was standing and leaning against a table, and heard some one say, "I arrest you." I looked around and saw that the conversation was addressed by a man I afterwards learned was Moffat to a young Mexican. I did not know Moffat at the time. I had never seen him before that time to my knowledge. I did not know the Mexican's name, and don't think I had ever spoken a dozen words to him in my life. I had seen him occasionally playing at some games in the saloon. I had also seen him at St. Louis, Sierra county, some time before, when I was there sick. He was brought into the hotel at St. Louis, where I was stopping, to be taken care of. He had been cut by a Spanish woman. I was just able to get out of my bed. Hearing there was a man cut, I went into his room and saw he was a Mexican. He told me what was the matter, which was about all the conversation we had. Some time after, he came to Downieville, and asked me, in Spanish, how I got along. I told him I was well, and simply asked him if he had recovered from his wound. This is all I recollect of ever saying to the Mexican. I may have spoken to him at some other time, but, if so, don't recollect it.

After Moffat said the words above related, Blackhawk, another Mexican, well-known in Downieville, and still living there, asked Moffat, if he believed the Mexican was a thief, why he did not get a warrant and have him arrested. Moffat then asked if there was anybody in the house that knew the Mexican. I spoke, and said that I had seen him at St. Louis, sick, some time before that. I then understood Moffat to say to me that he would not take my word for anything—that he wanted nothing to do with me, nor any of my band. My reply to Moffat was that I did not belong to any band. I think that Moffat then turned and went out into the front room. I then remarked either, "I wonder what he meant," or "that is no good way to talk to a man"—something to that effect. I did not know where he had gone. I wondered that an entire stranger should talk that way to me, when I answered civilly a question of his own asking. I did not know his business, or why he wished to arrest the Mexican, and never heard the reason until I was tried at Nevada. In from three to five minutes, I went into the front room. I had no intention of following him, did not know he was there, and did not think of ever speaking to him again. Just as I went out of the back room, I met with Jacob Rediker, the keeper of the saloon. I spoke to him and said, "Let us take a drink." While standing at the bar, waiting for our drinks, it struck me to tell Rediker what had been said to me in the back room. I remarked to him, I think, "What big shoulder-striker is that around calling everybody thief?" Rediker replied, "He is no shoulder-striker," and advised me not to notice anything that had been said; to let it go—that he was a miner. We took our drinks. Rediker started into the back room. I turned around and saw a number of men standing together, and did not know, at the time, what the gathering amounted to.

After stepping up to the crowd, to see what was going on, I saw Moffat talking to the Mexican. I did not know before that he was there, but walked up out of curiosity, because I heard loud talking. I did not press into the crowd, but was about three feet from Moffat when I stopped. His back was partially towards me, so that I saw the side of his face, but did not catch his eye; and he could not see me. I stood about a minute hearing the conversation; Moffat then looked over his shoulder directly at me—looking me full in the eye, with an angry expression of countenance. I had not spoken a word, or moved from my place. Looking me in the eye, he asked me:—"Who are you looking at?" I replied, "I am looking at you." He said, "I don't want you to look at me." I said, "You must certainly take me for a thief?" He said, "I do think you are a thief, and belong to a band of robbers." He looked directly at me, and I heard him distinctly make that remark. I said, "Take that back," at the same time drawing my pistol. He said, "He would take back nothing for none of my kind." When he made that remark I seemed to turn partially blind; I was bewildered with passion; the liquor I had drank, and his offensive manner and remarks, that I felt to be unjust, urged me to strike at him, which I did, with the muzzle of the pistol. I thought of the pistol, and used it, only as something to strike with; I did not shoot, and did not draw it for that purpose. If I had intended to shoot, and not strike him, I could have done so at once. I did not hit him. The blow was backhanded. He dodged back, and the blow missed him. He then stepped forward, and I struck a downward blow at him; I don't think the pistol struck him, though it may have grazed his arm. As I made the last blow, I stepped one step forward with my left foot, but did not move my right. He dodged as I struck, and described about a half circle, and closed in towards me. I was too much intoxicated to have the full use of my strength, and did not move as rapidly as if I had been sober.

As he closed towards me, he grabbed for the pistol. He afterwards declared he did not get hold of the pistol; I don't know whether he did or not. If he did not, I don't know how it went off. I did not cock it or aim it. As he grabbed for it, I caught it with my left hand, and the motion may have involuntarily knocked back the cock. As it discharged, I had the pistol grasped in both hands, about the butt, to keep him from pulling it out of my hands. The best of my opinion and recollection is, that he did get hold of the pistol by the muzzle, and that it discharged as he pulled it. Whether or not he pulled it, or it was discharged by my excited movements, I am equally guiltless of any intention to take the life of Moffat. This I firmly declare, in view of the accountability to which I am rapidly approaching, and after all motive has passed away to state anything but the truth of that miserable affray. After the discharge of the pistol, I stood for a moment benumbed. I did not know he was hit; whether the ball had gone into him, or any other, or into the ceiling. As I thus stood, I felt a slight push from some one, and was told I had shot a man, and to leave.

In reference to this affair I have this to say: Had I been sober,

A VIEW OF DOWNIEVILLE.

I should never have drawn a pistol, or used it; but sober, or not, I should at all hazards to myself have deeply resented an insult like that heaped upon me. I was peculiarily sensitive to such an insult. Had I never fallen into gambling habits, and thus tarnished my good name, I might have felt sustained by my own rectitude, and public knowledge of me, under aspersions as serious; but, conscious that my associations were against me, I could not but feel acutely the public declarations of a man who accused me of things I felt entirely innocent of, and which might yet be believed, because I was a gambler. I had never talked with a robber, Mexican or otherwise, had never had anything to do with one, and had never stolen a dollar in my life. When Moffat pronounced me a thief, the accusation flashed on my mind like lightning, and hence the occurrence. I did not intend to kill; I had only a blind determination to give him a beating that I thought he deserved. He was a powerful man, far my superior in strength, and viewed in the light of the testimony on the trial, in justice to myself, it must be admitted that he urged a drunken man beyond the bounds of reason, and his fate was natural, even if I am not clear of all criminal act.

I have never denied that I was the cause of his death, though unintentionally, but I claimed of the zeal that crowded me to an ignominious end, to weigh the circumstances in which I was placed by his inconsiderate acts, and so far as he was blameworthy, to lighten me of responsibility. He had abundant opportunity to escape. I leveled no pistol at him, all the witnesses declare. He insulted me grossly, and then crowded upon me. I can see no justification for his acts; he was entirely sober, and had he acted as a reasonable man, would now be alive. I can but look upon him as the author of his own fate and mine.

There was not a word spoken from the time I was pushed and told to go, until I got into the street; when in the street, I was told to run. The person who told me to go, kept with me as I ran up street, and turned the corner of the United States Hotel. We went up the mountain-side some two hundred yards, when I remarked to the man with me, that I was so sick I could not walk. He said he was afraid of compromising himself in the eyes of the law, and that we were both in great danger, if the matter was as bad as we feared. I asked him to stay by me until I was sober, unless the crowd came up that way, in which case to look out for his own safety. I washed my head in a brook, and vomited severely. We then went over through Cayoteville to the St. Louis trail, and he said he would go back and find out how bad the matter was, and come back and tell me. While he was gone, I sat on a rock near the trail. He came back about two o'clock at night, and said he was afraid it was a very bad case, and that they

DEATH OF MOFFAT.

would hang me if they caught me. He brought a friend with him. We talked over what was best to do. I told them that I would be my own counsel in getting away. They did not persuade or particularly advise me in any way, but proposed to assist me in any way they could. The proposition was made to get a mule and money, and then I would look out for myself. One of them went with me, and the other started for the mule and money. The one left with me and I started and traveled very slowly, most of the time on the St. Louis trail, using great precaution. When about half a mile from Eureka, we heard a man coming whistling. We went off the road. This was about daylight. We thought it unsafe to travel, and so camped in the chapparel that day, with nothing to eat. We lay there until about sundown, and then started on towards St. Louis, passing through the edge of Eureka, well towards the top of the mountain at Craig's Flat. We were much fatigued, and went a few steps off the road and laid down to rest. While lying there, we heard men coming on horseback. When they came within hearing, I recognized their voices as those of friends, and did not hesitate to speak to them. They dismounted at once, and gave me and my wearied friend their animals. We rode slowly until we got up to within a few hundred yards of Craig's Flat, and then gave back the animals, and the owners went to seek for some food for us. We went to the left of Craig's Flat, some distance out of town, and were to stop at the foot of Craig's Flat hill and wait for our friends. This was about two o'clock of the second night. To that place our friends brought us some crackers and cheese, and some liquor—the first food we had had since leaving Downieville. We then kept on the road to St. Louis; when within about two miles of that place, I took to the chapparel again, with one of my friends. In about two hours I had several visitors of my friends, and got the general news. I stayed there next day, within a few rods of the road. All through that day I was visited by a great many of my friends, and knew everybody that was after me, and saw several of them. When night came on we started for St. Louis; my friend walked about sixty yards ahead. There was no danger of anybody surprising me from behind, because I could have heard them coming, while his walking before, had anybody been on the lookout ahead, would have led them to spring out on him, and I could take care of myself on hearing the scuffle. As no one but friends knew that he was with me, his being taken could do no harm to him. I recognized all my friends by a peculiar whistle.

Within about a half mile of St. Louis, my friends met me with provisions, and an animal to leave with. After getting on my mule, and being advised by some of my friends to use precaution, I was told that there was a man there who would go with me, who knew the country. I had had little acquaintance with this man, but took him on this recommendation. This was about nine o'clock of the third night. We started at once, and went that night to American Valley. After seeing me safe through American Valley, he told be there was no danger if I would use precaution, and said I would have to pick my way from there; that he knew no more of the country than I did from that point. I went on that day after he left me, and crossed Feather River. There I fed my mule, and laid down and took a nap. I stopped that night at Brush Creek. Next morning I started out, rode all that day, the next night, and the following day till eleven o'clock—a distance of two hundred and thirty-five miles—and stopped near Shasta. The men with whom I stopped near Shasta told me the distance. During all this long ride I had no food for my mule, and was compelled to keep clear of the settlements, and thus go much out of my way, to keep ahead or clear of the news. Near Shasta, I met the stage bound down, and saw as many as three men on it that I was intimately acquainted with, and two others on foot, but was not recognized by any of them. I did not think the news was ahead of me at that time. I went into Shasta, put up my mule at a livery stable and thought I would look around and see if the news had got there. I was there but a few minutes, when I learned that the news had got in there that night. After supper, there were several newspapers brought to the hotel where I stopped. Thinking the landlord looked rather suspiciously at me, I told him the mule belonged to a man there at that place, and that I would go and

A street scene in Shasta City.

look the man up, and that when he came for the mule, to let him have it. I started out to look for a friend, and soon found one, and sent him for the mule. I went to a little town five miles from Shasta, on the road to Yreka, and stayed next day. I traveled directly on the road from there to Scott's Bar; I got at Scott's Bar the evening after it was burnt. I made no stop there, and went to French Bar. At that place I found a number of friends. I was told that the news was there, and it was best not to stop. I cannot now conceive how the news traveled so fast. I rode one of the best animals in the State, scarcely stopping to get anything to eat; yet the news was in French Bar the night before I got there. Here a friend, or pretended friend, advised me to ride on slowly. I took the reverse of his advice; and rode on as rapidly as I could. The Express started for Crescent City the day before the fire, from Scott's Bar, and I the day after; but I got into Crescent City before the Express, and told the news of the fire. When the expressman got in, he called me a liar, and was going to whip me for saying the town had been burnt; but about an hour after the news was confirmed. I think the expressman's name was Jackson. A man by the name of Stewart confirmed my story.

At Crescent City, I traded off my mule for a half-breed Indian animal, and got sixty-five dollars to boot. I then started up the coast, traveling twenty-five miles that day. I thought I would seek shelter in a small frame house a few rods from the road. When I hailed the occupant, he made his appearance. I recognized him as one of my neighbor-boys at home; he did not know me. I told him my real name, but did not tell him of my trouble. He was very anxious to have me stay with him, but I made an excuse that I wanted to get into Oregon before the rainy season set in. The next night I stopped at a hotel on Chetco River, with a man by the name of Miller. His wife spoke the "jargon" fluently, and told me all the Indian troubles they had had for four years past. There was much talk of an Indian war, and of the danger of traveling. I had now got beyond the news of myself, and think I should have been in no danger had I staid there until this time. This location is the prettiest spot I have ever seen in California or Oregon. It is at the mouth of the river, on the coast, and on a high knoll. I was told almost incredible accounts of the productiveness of the soil.

The next night I stopped at Rogue River; I stopped with a lady there whose husband had been two days before killed by soldiers, because he had shot at an Indian in the soldiers' charge. The next night I stopped twenty-two miles above the mouth of Rogue River, with a man who a few nights afterwards was murdered by the Indians. I then went to Port Orford, and stopped a few miles out of the place about a week. The steamer landed at that place from San Francisco, and I did not know but that somebody who knew me might be on it, and therefore did not stop in town. After leaving there, I traveled one day, and stopped a week on Chetco River, with a man by the name of Jones. He persuaded me to stay with him, said that there were bad Indians there, and that he would be happy of my company. The fourth morning after I was there, five Indians came in and commenced an assault by kicking over the oven in which he had his bread. One of them at the same time clinched him, and drew a knife. He called on me to assist him, telling me to help him till he could get hold of his pistol. The Indians did not molest me. I laid hold of the Indian, and jerked them apart. After Jones got hold of his pistol, I let

A HOMESTEAD IN NORTHERN CALIFORNIA.

the Indian go, and told Jones to use his pistol, and not stand with it in his hand, till the Indian got hold of him again. The Indian did not seem to fear him, but rushed for him, and grabbed the pistol. In the scuffle the pistol went off, the ball lodging in the floor. The Indian being too powerful for Jones, threw him down. Jones told me to save him if I could. At this time, the Indian struck at him with the pistol; I caught the blow on my hand, making a considerable bruise, which was sore for three months after. I wrung the pistol out of the Indian's hand, and knocked him down. Upon that, two other Indians started at me, and I served them the same way. Seeing the matter was getting desperate, I got my six-shooter and bowie knife out of the bed. When the Indians saw the big knife, they threw up their hands and said they did not want to fight. They went to the outside of the house, and then asked Jones if I was his friend, and said that when I left there they would kill him. I left next morning, and afterwards heard that the Indians did kill Jones, but don't know whether it was so or not.

I started for Cammas (?) Valley. The road is a mere elk track, and for hours I wandered around among dead trees, briars and undergrowth. About sundown of that day, as it was raining very hard, I met a California lion. He gave a loud, rough growl at me, and I felt my hair standing up on my head, raising my hat. I spoke aloud: "Old fellow, if you will let me alone, I will let you alone; for if we fight, and you win the fight, there will be nobody left to tell the tale." I stood, with my pistol in my hand a few minutes, when he left. I was determined not to commence the fight, and if he did, I meant to win if I could. I was much relieved by seeing him trot off. About two miles farther, I saw a small fire; determined to find out the cause, I went to it. It was now very dark and rainy. I found one man at the fire; he asked me a great many questions. My opinion of him was, that he had fled from justice. He told me he was formerly from Ohio, where he had a wife and two children, and never expected to go back there again. I told him nothing of my life, and he nothing more to me of his. I stayed with him all night. I left him in the morning, and traveled all day through a heavy rain. That evening, about sundown, I came in sight of Cammas Valley. It took me till about an hour after dark to get down into the valley. Down in the valley, I went to a house and found no one there, but plenty of chickens. Not feeling disposed to enter the house, I started to find one where somebody lived. I had a similar luck at three other houses. I could not account for this, but started on. About five miles far-

Salem, Oregon.

ther, I came to a house, and found some sixteen or eighteen men fortified, to protect themselves against the Indians. Their families had all left the valley, and gone to Roseburg. I staid with them all night. They told me awful stories of the danger of traveling from Indians, but I started on down the valley the next morning. I traveled on for five days, without particular incident, until I arrived at Salem. At Salem, I inquired for the residence of Giles Dougherty, an old friend of my father. I found him about five miles from Salem, across the river. He received me kindly, and to him I related all the circumstances of the affair at Downieville, and my subsequent travels. He was much incensed at Moffat calling me a thief, and did not wonder at my killing him under the circumstances. I found, on inquiry, that many of my father's and my friends were located in the neighborhood. Dougherty had three sons in the wars. I told him, that if there was another call for volunteers, I would like to enlist, and would do so. I spent a month with my friends there, and enjoyed myself. They were men in good standing, and did all they could to lighten my cares. My conscience did not accuse me of intentional homicide, however Moffat might have come out of the affair. I did not know his fate, but my sincere prayer was for his recovery.

In a month a call was made for recruits, and I enlisted in Captain Hardin's Company. This was in February, 1856. There were about ninety men in the Company, recruited at Salem. We went, at once, by land, to Fort Dalles, by way of Portland, at which latter place we stopped a week. While stopping there the volunteers called on the officers to treat. The officers did so, and the men became pretty well stimulated with liquor. Shortly after, a man

THE DALLES: NEZ PERCE INDIANS IN FOREGROUND.

by the name Edes, a member of our Company, had a difficulty with a half-breed, a weakly and rather inoffensive man. Corporal Grigsby, a good-natured, excellent young man, interfered and requested Edes to desist, and told him good humoredly that if he wanted to have a fight to take hold of some one of his size, at the same time taking hold of Edes and turning him around, laughing as he did so. Edes at once drew a knife, and plunged it into Grigsby. Grigsby died in twenty-four hours. Edes was delivered over to the civil authorities, tried, and convicted of murder in the second degree, and sentenced to the Penitentiary for life.

At the Dalles we stayed about a week, and then started for headquarters, in Walla-walla Valley, where we joined the regiment, under command of Col. Cornelius. We stayed there some three weeks, and elected a Major. We hung one Indian who came in as a spy and was detected. We then started for Snake River, and were two days and a half on the route. At this time we received fresh horses, from the Nez Perce Indians. At Snake River there were a number of Indians encamped on the opposite side. As the volunteers came up on the knoll, by the river, in sight of the Indian camp on the opposite side, they did not wait for the word of command, but some of them pulled off three boats that were on the wagons, and launched them into the river. Others fired across the river with their muskets, a distance of three hundred yards, while the boats were getting ready. The volunteers then crossed the river, and charged on the encampment, killing five Indians and dispersing the rest. I rushed in with the others, but don't think I killed any Indians. I do not think any officer was on that side of the river until after the Indians were routed. We had been on less than half rations for about five days. At the encampment we found, in *caches*, about twenty-five bushels of corn, and a quantity of cammas roots. The men were half famished, and it was amusing to see them greedily knawing large pieces of this root. The Indians cook the root by a steaming process, and we found a considerable quantity of it ready cooked. It has a taste much resembling liquorice. We also found several chickens, which were at once cooked and devoured. The Indians were scalped, and left unburied. Any one who killed an Indian scalped him. Some half-breeds put the scalps on poles, and had a war-dance about them, in which pastime the Americans did not participate.

This point is about ten miles above where the Snake River empties into the Columbia. A flat spreads back from the river to the foot of the mountain, of about twenty acres, composed of a sandy soil, covered with an inferior grass. At the back of the flat the mountain rises abruptly to the height of a mile. The mountain is also composed of a white, clayey sand. The surface is slightly colored with grass. All over the side of the mountain are trails made by Indian horses, resembling net-work, shining white in the sun, and appearing from the flat, like an artificial work, so regular and beautiful is the netting of trails. As the Indians on the flat caught the alarm of our approach they signaled to the Indians on the side of the mountain, who were herding some four or five hundred head of horses; these, taking the alarm, ran the horses full speed down the hill to the camp, to furnish the Indians in the camp animals to escape with. It was a most beautiful and exciting scene to see the horses rushing under the urgency of the whip at full speed down the trails, neighing and plunging together, of all colors, with the shouting

Indians compelling them on. It resembled a living panorama, which our own impetuous motions did not prevent me from enjoying. The next morning some of the officers and about seventy-five men went out to scout the country for Indian camps. I was not with them, but heard the officers' accounts when they returned. They traveled through the heavy sand to the mouth of Snake river, and there found about one hundred Indians, including squaws and children. The Indians at once launched their canoes, piled them full, and put out into the river. As our men got to the river-side they fired, killing some Indians and splitting several canoes. The inmates swam to the opposite shore, and little children three years old, and old squaws, succeeded in reaching it, a mile distant, through the extremely cold water. The river at this point is very rapid, and tasks to the utmost the powers of a horse to swim it.

As I was not on guard, and had nothing in particular to do, while this company were gone, I took my musket and climbed the mountain in search of rabbits, or to scout Indians on my own hook. Not finding either, I took the Indian horses for game, and shot several of them, creeping upon them and firing. I was about ten miles from camp during the excursion, but encountered none of the dangers that everybody was talking of in that region. The next day the party returned, and the day after the whole command were allowed to rest. Some of us, however, started out for Indian horses. We captured about one hundred head—driving them into a sharp bend in the river, where there was a high bluff, and lassooing them. It was rare sport; sometimes a man would capture a horse, and after saddling and mounting him, would be thrown off, the horse starting away full speed, head up, proud of his achievement. In such case the owner of the saddle would get his musket, and hunt down and shoot the horse, to get back his property. On the fourth day we received orders from head-quarters to go to Peluse river, forty miles distant. We traveled up Snake river, on a narrow trail, sometimes wandering high up the mountains, over a rough, craggy country, expecting to find an army of Indians at Peluse river, waiting our arrival. When there we saw no fresh sign of Indians. The Peluse river is a small stream, with deep gulches covered with loose, shelly rock, and is about the size of the Yuba. We traveled up about seven miles from the mouth to the falls. Here we found a small valley, and encamped to recruit our animals, and to scout for Indians. The valley is of about twelve acres. At its foot is a perpendicular fall of, as I estimated, two hundred feet, though others deemed it higher. The water plunged into a basin of rock, worn out at the base. A stone, of the size of a man's head, let fall, was at once dashed out of the basin by the force of the water. It was a magnificent sight.

From here scouts were sent out all over the country. On the second day we were nearly out of provisions. On the third the Colonel and some of his men ran in between forty and sixty fat horses. The boys all being hungry did not wait for an invitation, but grabbed their guns and began shooting fat horses. While some were selecting a horse to ride, others were skinning one to prepare him for supper. In one hour I think there were eleven horses skinned and dressed. The men had set off in messes of six, with a pack mule to each mess. Some of the messes had a little flour to make soup, but the one to which I belonged had nothing but horse meat "straight," without salt. After living

Fort Walla-Walla.

three days on this food, the men got dissatisfied and threatened to leave unless steps were taken to save them from starvation. A meeting was held, at which some of the men resolved on leaving the next morning, and built a raft on Snake River for that purpose. But before starting on the raft, some wagon loads of provisions came in sight and the trouble was over. I must admit I had my share in these proceedings and determined to go, although the Colonel threatened to shoot us all as deserters. But I could not see the propriety of keeping us there inactive, away from Indians or settlements, living on noisome food, while he had bread, and told him my musket had fourteen pistol balls in it, and I thought I could fight my way through. Luckily there was not occasion for such a desperate result. I was willing to fight Indians, but not to stay where no fighting was to be done, and live on horse meat.

At this time an order was made for some twenty-seven men to go to Walla-walla, and the rest were to go to Priest Rapids on the Columbia. I went with the former party. The party to Priest Rapids traveled about one hundred and fifty miles over a sandy plain without water or grass, except a poison spring which proved fatal to a great many of the horses. On that trip about one hundred and seventy horses were left on this desert, besides a great many saddles and other property. The horses had been appraised in the volunteer service at from three to four hundred dollars each—fine American horses. The suffering in this objectless trip was immense, and the cost to the government very heavy. No Indians were found there, and none had been there for some time. On their arriving at the Rapids there was little grass, and provisions were scarce; so the party made its way as fast as possible down the Columbia to Walla-walla, the head-quarters. On the way down they saw an old gray headed Indian behind a rock. Some one cried "Indians," and shot at him. He fell back and when the men went up to him it was found the ball had grazed the top of his head. He was in a pitiable situation. The boys gave him what they could spare, and left him to worry his life out among the rocks. He gave them all the information he could about the war party of the Indians. The Colonel's command kept down the Columbia till they got to the mouth of Snake River, when they met the Clackamas company, who assisted them with boats across the river. The Colonel then took three hundred men and went down on the Washington side, while the rest of us came down the Oregon side to Walla-walla, about twelve miles below the mouth of Snake River, under command of Major Burton.

I knew nothing more of the Colonel's party until they got to Fort Dalles. He had between three and four hundred head of horses. At that place the Indians charged on the guard that had the care of the horses, took the guns that were hanging to the saddles, and ran off the horses. The guards were listlessly loitering about. The horses were never regained. No one was killed in the stampede.

Our company of twenty-seven went on to Walla-walla and camped, having come from Peluse River, as we were ordered. At this place we found a part of our regiment who had started directly from Cornelius Camp for this place. They had been here some three weeks when we arrived. We had been there some four weeks when the Priest Rapids party arrived. At the mouth of Walla-walla River, some three miles below where we were encamped, stood an old Hudson Bay Co. Fort, much dilapidated. In the Columbia at that point we descried an old iron English cannon, weighing some seven hundred pounds. We put our lassoes around it, dragged it up on the bank, and found it was pounded full of stones. We built a large fire around it and thoroughly dried it, and then pricked as much powder as we could into the touch hole. A large party of Indians on the other side of the river, out of rifle range, were watching our proceedings, dancing about, making gestures at us, and halloing. They knew we had no boats, and did not seem to understand our movements. When all was ready, we touched the infernal machine off with a long cedar torch. The stones rattled across the river among the Indians, up on to the hill sides, changing their mirth into consternation, and clearing the vicinity of red skins as fast as legs or horse-flesh could carry them. In a few minutes there was not an Indian to be seen. I don't know what the bill of mortality was; but that was the last we saw of Indians in that neighborhood.

We lay at the Walla-walla country until the Colonel arrived on the opposite side of the Columbia. We did not join him again, but kept down the river on the Oregon side. We went next to Fort Henrietta, on the U-mah-ti-lah river. Here our captain was allowed to take his company under his special command, and was ordered to encamp above the Fort. After being there three days we went scouting to the mouth of the U-mah-ti-lah, and saw a party of Indians on the other side. We fired across at them and returned. The next morning we received news that the Indians

A CAVALRY PATROL IN THE MOUNTAINS.

had attacked the Fort, killed the guard, and stolen about one hundred head of horses, and we were ordered to immediately pursue them. The captain on hearing the news ordered twenty-seven of his best men to mount the best horses in the camp. This was done in a very few minutes. I was selected to go with the party. In twenty minutes we were off, the Indians having some six miles the start of us. After riding half a mile, we surmounted the ridge, and saw the Indians about six miles ahead, on a large plain. We dashed on at a break-neck speed, all having fine horses, the captain leading the way, and the rest keeping up as near abreast as possible. The Indians were also mounted upon fine horses. They drove the stolen horses on ahead of them, and had the advantage of us, in that they could change their tired horses for fresh ones whenever they pleased. I had started off in such a hurry that I had on no hat or boots. As we neared a place called Butter Creek we got to within a mile of the Indians, who seemed to be making fun of us. The captain here saw that the body of Indians was not very large, and selected ten men having the best horses to go with him, and left the rest of us in charge of the lieutenant to come on more slowly, so as not to tire our horses. But we were too impatient for such counsels, and pushed on at nearly the speed of the captain's party. My horse was a splendid one, the best in the party, though the captain did not know it. As the captain's party got to the creek, a great body of Indians concealed there, rose up at once and gave fight to the advance party of our men, compelling them to slack up. The rest of us were only a few hundred yards behind, and were there in a moment. The Indians then dashed across the creek, and we charged up to it, and found a bluff bank ten feet high, covered with sour grass as high as the horses' backs, and no sign of a trail or crossing place. The great body of the Indians formed on the other side to keep us from crossing, while a few pushed ahead with the stolen horses. We fired at them, but could not cross or find where they had crossed. The captain kept searching up and down the river to find a trail. I fired my gun, and at the moment discovered that the top of my powder flask was gone and the most of the powder spilt. I felt very savage, and ran up and down the river to get across. The bluff looked terribly high and steep. At that moment a man said to me, "why don't you cross, are you afraid of the Indians?" I was enraged at the remark and dashed over the bank, and nearly got drowned; but my horse bore up bravely. As I got upright, I called to the man and said, "why don't you come on, you coward?" He did not follow me. By this time the captain had found a place to cross, and got over with some ten men. We charged on to the Indians, and killed some twenty-seven horses on the knoll and in the running fight immediately after. We did not know whether we killed Indians or not, but must have done so, as we saw tracks of Indian blood all along the hills. When we fired, and an Indian or his horse fell, another Indian would catch the Indian by the hair and draw him up on his horse before or behind him, to save his scalp. By that means they took their dead and wounded with them. We chased the Indians, every one making the best speed he could. Many of the horses gave out and the men fell behind; but my horse seemed to like the excitement as well as I did, and got better and better.

We kept up a running fight for some ten miles. I was continually passing others of our men who were giving out, seeing that there were some yet left with me. We rode on at the top of our speed for some three miles, not firing a shot. By this time I became so excited I neither knew nor cared whether any of the company were along or not. I wanted a red man's scalp, and tried all I could to get in reach of one with my pistol, knife, or gun, or any thing I could use to capture it. I soon discovered that I was alone, and a mile ahead of the captain and all but one or two men. I was in gun shot of the Indians when I found there were but two men in my sight—one on foot whose horse had given out, and one a friendly Indian. The man on foot was about two hundred yards behind me, when an Indian ahead, addressed me in the Indian language, "how are you, sir," telling me at the same time to come up and he would fight me. I told him that he was a "cowardly son of a b—." He replied back to me in plain English, the same remark. Upon that I discharged my musket at him at a distance of two hundred and fifty yards. The shot struck the horse, and the red skin was obliged to leave him. At the same time fifteen or twenty of his party joined him from behind a hill, and advanced rapidly towards me, charging down on their horses. I gave way, and retreated until I came to the man on foot behind me and there made a stand. I would have died rather than have left him. The Indians charged to within pistol shot of us, and I fired all the barrels of my six shooter and he his rifle. More of our men appearing in sight at the moment, the Indians again retreated. The captain at this moment came up and ordered all the men whose horses had given out, to form a body and go back. I remarked to the captain that my animal was just getting good. We pursued the Indians to Willow Creek. There we rested an hour or two, and the Indians a mile or two ahead did the same, moving when we did. We pursued them till sundown, when we lost sight of them. We had no provisions whatever, but made a "dry camp" for the night. Myself and another man went out about half a mile and found an Indian mare that had been shot. We killed it, and took part of the ribs and inwards into camp and roasted them. I eat heartily of this food, though some of the men preferred hunger. We then went out on the hills and dug the roots used by the Indians, that we had learned to know, by the tops, were not poisonous, and eat them that night. Next morning we started back. That day our lieutenant was taken sick, and we had to camp to wait for his recovery. The next day at noon, we arrived at Butter Creek, and met some twenty-five men with provisions for us. It was about three days from the time we left camp at the U-mah-ti-lah, before we had anything fit to eat. We then retraced our trail, and started for Eureka Valley. Getting at the foot of the Black Mountains we found the Indians had turned and gone to the Columbia River. We saw nothing more of them.

In the exciting fight I have described, I neither thought nor cared for death. At one time, as I stood by the lieutenant, with my hand on his saddle, a slug from an Indian's gun took out a piece of the horse's jaw, and passed under my arm. I heard the balls whistle all around me. Sometimes I would chase an Indian a mile, with no charge in my gun. I had none in it when I leaped over the bluff into the creek. I tried only to get near enough to the Indians to get a scalp, and depended on my knife to gain one, if I could catch the Indian. The Indians put into their guns small pieces of iron log chains, or any iron slugs they could get hold of. They are very bad marksmen. They used the Hudson Bay

Co.'s smooth bore guns. Not one of our men was injured in all this savage chase.

At the foot of the mountains a heavy snow storm came on. We followed Indian trails over a rough country, until we came to the road from the Dalles to Fort Henrietta, and returned to the fort, where we lay a short time, and then were ordered to Fort Dalles, about the last of April, 1856. On the 5th of May I took my discharge, and stopped at the fort about three weeks. I then hired to a man to cut saw logs, fifteen miles from the fort. He told me he wanted me to drive an ox team to his mill; at the same time another team was going. We started, the other team ahead, and two men with it. It would take till night to reach the mill. At noon we reached Ten Mile Creek, and unhitched the

ON THE COLUMBIA RIVER.

oxen. The other men had their dinners with them, and I nothing to eat. They eat very composedly, I sitting by, and did not offer me a scrap. I was extremely hungry, and incensed. We hitched up the cattle again, and I soon managed to tip over my wagon, at the same time forgetting to hallo "whoa" to the oxen. The men said they wanted no such ox-driver; I told them I wanted no such companions. At this time, a man came up with a drove of horses, going to Willamette Valley, and offered me good pay to go with him. I consented. I told the men to give my respects to my employer, and tell the "old buck" that I was not a very good ox-driver. I staid with my new employer at the creek some two days, and started on the third with fifty head of horses, besides colts. We traveled to the Cascade mountains, and in crossing them found snow some fifteen feet in depth. In some places, there was a crust on it that bore up the horses, in others it was very soft. We were three days going fifteen miles. These mountains are heavily timbered with pine and fir. While on the mountains, a boy with us reported he had seen a black bear. I started out with my musket to find the bear, and soon discovered him. The bear started for the brush, and I tried to shoot at him, but the charge in the musket was wet, and wouldn't go off. Intent on capturing him, I ran after him, discharging my six-shooter, but he got away. The country abounds in bears, deer, and other game.

We soon got into Willamette Valley, where I employed my time in breaking-in wild horses, catching them and saddling them, and often getting thrown off, only to catch the same one or another to try the same experiment. The owner of the horses was meanwhile engaged in trading the horses for cattle. We

Oregon City, in the Willamette Valley.

traveled up the north side of the valley to Eugene City, and down on the south side to Salem, where my friends lived, and where I had enlisted. The man I made this last trip with was called "Mountain Jackson." I left him at Salem. This was about the last of June, 1856. I stopped with my friends the remainder of June. I then saddled up my horse, and left a note sticking on a tree at Doak's Ferry, to the effect that I was going to French Prairie to spend the Fourth of July. I went to Canemah, where I sold my animal, and took a steamboat and went to Oregon City the same night, and next day to Portland. After one night in Portland, I went to Fort Vancouver, and got there the 3rd of July. There were great preparations for the 4th. About ten o'clock of the 4th, I was standing in the street, and a man told me he thought I was the man who wanted to fight him for a dollar and a half. The street was crowded with gentlemen and ladies. I told him I was not, and tried to excuse myself, and to get away from him. He insisted that I was, and that we must have the fight out. I told him I was *not* the man. He called me a liar, and I knocked him down, and kicked him for falling. I got more credit for that than anything else I did in Oregon. He was a well-known bully. This was the first dispute or difficulty I had had since leaving Downieville. On the 6th, I went to Fort Dalles. On the 11th, I commenced work for the Government, under charge of Quartermaster Jourdan. I hired to pack provisions to Fort Yakima. The distance between the two places is about sixty miles, over a rough, mountainous country. I packed provisions about a month. At the end of that time, I started with Capt. Russell, with a pack train for Fort Walla-walla, by way of the Yakima River. While we were encamped on a tributary of that river, one evening, one of the soldiers was, or pretended to be, crazy, and struck one of his companions with an ax, striking him from behind, cutting his

Fort Vancouver.

jugular vein and collar bone; repeating the blow with the poll of the ax, breaking his skull. We buried the victim, and took the murderer with us to stand his trial.

Arriving at the Columbia, at the old Hudson Bay Co.'s fort, we being on the opposite, or Washington Territory side, we used india-rubber boats to cross, and swam our animals. While crossing with the last load of pack saddles, in an old canoe which had been pressed into that service, the canoe split in two while in the middle of the river. There were twelve men on board of it, who clung to the pack saddles. The rubber boats were some one hundred yards off, and I at once went to their assistance. All the men were picked up, some nearly exhausted. The pack saddles were all lost. We went up the Walla-walla to a place where a fort was to be established, some forty miles from the mouth; we stayed there about two weeks. While there, the Indians came in to make a treaty with Gov. Stevens, who was then there for the purpose.

There were five companies of regulars there, under command of Col. Steptoe. About fifteen hundred Indians came in, mounted on horses, dressed in beads and paint, and other rude finery. All the regulars were formed in rank, and cannons fired, to exhibit to the Indians the power of the whites. When we left, we went to Fort Dalles with a wagon train—Capt. Russell commanding the train and guards. I had heretofore done no gambling, since leaving Downieville, but got into the habit again with the officers of this train. From Fort Dalles, we went again to Fort Walla-walla, where I took my discharge, having been in Government employ two months and nineteen days. I left the employ on the 1st of November, 1856. During the time I was with the wagon train, I was allowed by the wagon master to take goods and liquor on my own account, and out of them, with my wages, made some six hundred and fifty dollars, selling them to the soldiers. I had that sum of money when I got through.

I stopped at Fort Dalles, without employment, except an occasional game of cards, during the next month and a half. At the end of that time, I determined to go to the Colville mines. I had a partner, who furnished some horses, and I others. We packed eleven horses, taking two men and an Indian with us. We got as far on our road as Fort Walla-walla; there snow and rain set in. Finding we could sell our goods to the soldiers and Indians to good advantage, without permission of the Government, we commenced to sell them. Military law prevailed there, and such traffic was forbidden. In four days we had orders to leave, and to trade no more with the soldiers. The snow having fallen to considerable depth, we did not think it safe to go on, and returned towards Fort Dalles. When about fifteen miles from the fort, I had a dream that persons were there to take me, and would not go in, but went to Fifteen Mile Creek, sending the other men with a portion of the animals to the fort. The snow was all this time falling, and was thirty inches deep on the creek. I felt uneasy, and dispatched a man next night from Cox & Stoley's ranch, where I stopped, to find out if anybody was after me. I had heard nobody speak of the matter—it was only an impression arising from my dream. On his return, he informed me that there were persons there after me, but that no one knew at Fort Dalles that I had returned; and that my friends had given out that I had gone to the mines. Next day an Indian brought me a note from a friend at the fort, informing me that he did not think there was any danger, and that he would let me know if there was any.

A LITTLE TROUBLE IN CROSSING THE RIVER.

On New Year's night, I saddled up a horse, and went to the fort, to find out for myself. My friends said that they thought there was no danger, but I had better stay out on the ranch. On the night of the 12th, two of my friends came out to the ranch, and told me that they did not think there was any danger, but that I had better leave as soon as I could get away. I could not, however, get far into the upper country, at that season, on account of the deep snows. On the night of the 14th, I was very uneasy—got up and smoked my pipe about two o'clock, and thought I would leave and go to the Indians' camp. Being over-persuaded by one of the men in the cabin, I laid down and went to sleep. About daylight of the 15th, one of the men in the house got up and built a fire. About the time he had it built, some persons at the door called to have it opened. They said they wanted to warm themselves. The door was opened, and five men stood there. I was lying in my bed, my pistol under my head. I sprang up, knowing that the time had come for trouble. I jerked on my boots, and caught my pistol. One of the men said, "Jack, you are my prisoner." I did not speak, but partially presented my pistol, and at the same time was clinched by two of them, and the pistol wrenched from my hand. I tore myself loose from them, and ran for the door; at the same time one of them struck at my head with a six-shooter, the pistol discharging at the same moment. My mind was made up in a moment, to die rather than be disgraced with irons on my legs. I gained the outside of the door, in my shirt sleeves, and had nothing to defend myself with. One man, on the outside of the house, immediately discharged his pistol at me. I knew there was no chance to get away, but determined not to be taken alive, and ran to make them shoot at me. The snow was about two and a half feet deep. In running the distance of thirty yards, along a trail over which we were in the habit of going for water, some nine shots were fired at me. The last shot took effect about half an inch from the back bone, and came out about three inches below and to the left of the left nipple. A previous shot struck me in the thigh, though I did not feel it when it took effect. That shot afterwards gave me most trouble. Two other shots grazed me, but made no wounds. When the last shot took effect, I fell. My foes were but a few steps from me, and in a moment were where I was lying. One of them said—"Shoot the son of a b— again." My answer was, "I dare you to do it." They picked me up and took me to the house.

These men were pretty well drunk. After I was laid in the

"Flight of the Culprit," a contemporary sketch.

house, in my bunk, one of the men broke a bottle, and said, "Hurrah for hell, who cares for expenses." I spoke to Dr. Shogg, who was with them, and requested permission to stop for a while, that I felt I was dying. At the time I was numb, and bleeding very fast. He said I had got to go to Fort Dalles that night, dead or alive. In five minutes I was placed on a mule, a pair of handcuffs put on me by fastening one cuff on the wrist and the other to the horn of the saddle. They were pretty drunk, and went along halloing and laughing. I travelled some eight miles through the snow, the mule plunging, and sometimes falling, dragging me in the snow. They then loosed the handcuffs from the saddle. I was in as much pain as a man could bear and live, I think. At Olney's Ranch they took me from the mule, and I was conveyed from that place on a load of oats. After traveling some half a mile, the sledge turned over and I was buried in the snow. They reloaded the oats, dragged me up on them again, and we pursued our journey, arriving at Fort Dalles an hour before sun-down, and lodged me at Gate's Hotel, under guard.

I will here remark that, at the cabin, when the men came in the door, I heard some one say, "Boys, take him alive, if you can." At Olney's Ranch, when I was put on the sledge, they reloaded their pistols, and I noticed who did so. Jackson, one of their number, deputized from Siskiyou county to take me, held up his pistol and said, "See, boys, my pistol is as it was at the Dalles." I saw his pistol, and saw it was loaded, and knew he had not shot at me.

After arriving at the hotel, I was able to walk. My constitution was naturally good, and the hardships I had had in the mountains had made me very strong and rugged. Dr. Yates attended to my wounds. I lay there seventeen days. During that time I had sent for a lawyer to Portland. He informed me, through a friend, that he could take me away from the sheriff, and would do it if I would give him $1,000. In the course of the time I made a proposition to Jackson to buy my liberty. He told me he thought it would take more money than I had. I told him that I had some good friends who might possibly advance enough to be tempting to him. He told me that he had a price. I told him I would give him $1200 in cash. He studied a few minutes, and then told me he did not think that was enough. I asked him to set his price. He said he did not like to set a price unless he knew it would be kept a secret. I told him that if I could raise the money for him, that I would keep it a secret. After some hesitation, he told me $5,000. I could have got the money by sending to my friends in Willamette Valley, but I would not do it.

I was kindly cared for at the hotel. I still calculated upon the lawyer, but there was ice in the river at the time, so that he could not get from Portland. While at the hotel I was shackled on the legs, and had a handcuff on one wrist, the other cuff fastened to a trace-chain, and that fastened to the bed-rail by a padlock. On the eighteenth night, I unlocked the padlock with a little pocket-knife, while Jackson was drunk. He was the only guard, and had been drunk every night since we arrived in town. About 2 o'clock at night I got up, with nothing on but my under-clothes, and went out bare-footed into the snow, some two hundred yards up the street, and saw a man coming down towards me that I knew. I told him I wanted him to go and tell my friends that I had got away from Jackson, and that I wanted them to do something for me. Ten minutes from the time I left my bed I was in the saddle. My wounds were yet inflamed and running, my thigh was very bad, and it was almost death to me to ride. I put on a common loose, soldier's coat, without any shirt, and rode the remainder of that night, and got to Fifteen-mile Creek; there I swam my horse across the creek, pulled off my socks, and walked over on a log over which the water was running about eight inches deep. It was just daylight, and extremely cold. It commenced snowing very hard. I knew where some men were herding stock on the Deshutz river, and went to them. They took the irons off me, and one of them gave me a pair of shoes and twenty dollars. They told me it would not do for me to stay there; that the officers might find me, and they did not want to take the chance of appearing to conceal me from the law. One of them proffered to go with me to a large cañon, where I could stay until I got better, and that he would also bring me provisions. We went to the cañon, when I told him I was not satisfied with the place; that I wanted to cross the Deshutz river. We rested awhile, and then started down the river. At one place the mountain was so steep where we climbed it on our horses that my saddle slipped off backwards and I with it, both rolling down the hill. I was so weak I could not help myself much. Assisted by my friend, I managed to get to the top of the mountain. We travelled forwards about two miles. My friend then told me that if I would get off, he would fix my bed close to the bank of the river, in some brush, and go and find a canoe, some six miles below.

In about three hours I was called on by another friend, sent up by the one who went after the canoe. He asked me if I was able to go. I told him I was. We went to the canoe. It was very small, and dangerous crossing in it, but we got safely over. The white caps were rolling in the river, and it appeared impossible to cross it in such a conveyance. We camped near the river that night. The next day I was told that the Indian agent took great interest in having me captured, and had employed some three hundred Indians to search for me; that, in order to stimulate their exertions, he had told them that I had five hundred dollars with me, which they might have, and that he would give them five hundred dollars more. This I was told by an Indian that had worked for me. That night I went back over the river, had my horse saddled, and started by myself to strike the timber in the Cascade Mountains, thirty-five miles distant. I set out at about ten o'clock, and was four or five hours reaching the mountains. The night was dismal and cold; I was, however, warmly dressed, and had a good horse, but was in much misery from my wounds. I there turned out my horse, hid my saddle, took my blankets and started up the mountains afoot. After ascending three-fourths of a mile I was so much fatigued that I could not walk. I wrapped myself up in my blankets, laid down and slept. About an hour before sunset, I concluded to go to the top of the mountain, and when there, looking off in the valley, to the distance of about a mile, saw a house. I started to go to it, and got to within two hundred yards of it, when I saw two half-breed girls. On approaching them, I found they could not speak English, but told me they knew who I was, in the Indian tongue. They were the daughters of an old Frenchman, by an Indian woman. They said they knew I was the man who got shot. They told me there were Indians there hunting for me, who had followed my horse's tracks of the night before, and that they were then camped on the river three miles below. They told me if I would hide they would give me something to eat. They said, if they told their father about me, and told him not to tell upon me, that he would keep me concealed. They said I must come to the house; that the Indians were gone, and would not be back till next day; that they would give me something to eat, and show me where to hide. I did so, but after dark concluded to go to the mountain again. Before starting, they gave me some moccasins, so that the Indians might not know my tracks. I went about three miles that night. Next morning, I was told by an Indian boy, that I must "hide good," because there were lots of Indians after me. I went seven miles further into the mountains, and hid under a cliff of rocks, and dared not build a fire, for fear of attracting attention by the smoke. At night, I started to make my way back. When about three hundred yards of the house, about midnight, I found the owner waiting for me. He told me the Indians were there after me; that he would have to hunt me a better hiding-place; that they were all over the mountains; that if I could get on an island that was near there, I would be safe from the Indians. He gave me a loaf of bread, and I went to the island; the water was about waist deep. In the morning it commenced raining hard. I laid quiet all day, and at night waded out again. The old man gave me the general news, and something warm to eat, and I went back.

I kept up this course of life for thirteen days, wading out at night, after dark, getting provisions from my neighbor, and after talking with him for a few hours, would roll up in my blankets at the foot of a tree and sleep, and go back before daylight. It was seventeen days since I left the Deshutz river. On the seventeenth day I was visited by the old Frenchman and his two daughters, and told there were two horses left standing by the fence. I at once knew they were for me. He told me he would send his son with me, who knew all the Indians well, if I wished. We started about half an hour before dark next evening, and rode forty-six miles to the ferry on the Deshutz river, leaving Fort Dalles on the left. I rode in great pain. At the ferry I sent the boy to see if any of my enemies were there. The boy came back and told me there was nobody there but the ferryman. This was at daylight. I rode up and told the ferryman that I wanted to cross. He asked no questions. When on the other side I told him who I was. I knew he would tell that somebody had crossed there at daylight, and as there was little travel there, that I should be suspected; and I asked him to keep it to himself. He said he would do so, and gave me advice how to shun some travelers who were expected on the road. The boy left me at the ferry. I took a trail on the mountain, and went about two miles. The region is barren, and bare of timber. I stayed there that day till nearly sundown, and then saddled up one horse, and put my blankets on the other. I then started for the U-mah-ti-lah river, and lay on the ridge that night, in the frost.

John Day's river was the first I had to cross, and I was told I could ford it. I forced in the animal that carried the blankets, and found the water was swimming deep. The horse swam across and left me. I concluded to follow, and fastened my pistols to the horn of my saddle, and took off my shoes and coat. I found I could not force the animal I had been riding into the river. I then started up the same side of the river. After going up the river almost two miles, I came to some Indians. I asked them if they had any canoes. They said no, but they could send my things across on a rope, and fix a rope so that I could cross. There was a steep cliff of rocks on each side, and the stream was very swift. They got my things across, and fixed the rope for me. I started on the rope, when one of them let it loose, and I had to swim across. They let me fall about four feet into the water. My clothes and pistols were immediately taken by them. On reaching the other shore I was nearly frozen. My wounds were still very sore and painful. After getting out, the Indians gave me my coat and pants, but would not give me my shoes.

How I would like to go fighting Indians again! I started off barefoot. The Indians drew my pistols on me, and told me they would kill me. There were about twenty-five Indian men, and as many squaws and children. My only weapon was a rock, which I took in my hand, and started back to a fellow who had one of the pistols. I told him I wanted my pistol, and intended to have it. He said he intended to kill me with it. An old Indian woman told him not to shoot me. He then ran and hid the pistol. They told me I must stay with them that night. About 10 o'clock they tied me. They drew my feet close together and tied them—then tied my wrists together behind my back—then drew my hands as near to my feet as they could, and also tied my arms back as close to my shoulders as they could put the rope. I pretended to be very stiff, and thus kept them from getting my shoulders very near together, and also my hands down to my feet, knowing I could reach my feet, and untie the rope about my ankles. They then set an Indian woman to guard me. They roasted a salmon, a small piece of which they gave me, and then sang war songs. They sat round the fire and talked about what they would do in the morning. They would make me swim the river again, and if I drowned, it was all right. I heard them say that the Indian Agent had told them to kill me if I could not be taken otherwise. They were so anxious to get the reward, that they were disposed to take my life to be sure of it. It is perhaps needless to say that I understood their language perfectly. About 2 o'clock I untied the ropes, the guard sleeping soundly, or else, disposed to favor me, pretending to be asleep. I found the Indian women, in my general experience, very different from the men. They are far more gentle and humane. I got out of the hut without disturbing any of them. I had nothing on my feet but a pair of socks. I lost my way, and wandered over on to the Columbia. Before I got to the Columbia, a man might almost have tracked me by my blood. The sharp rocks cut through my socks, and my feet were covered with blood. Instead of going up the Columbia as I intended, in the dark, I went down the river. After traveling down almost seven miles, I came to a place where the bluff ran in so close to the river that I could not get round, and then discovered my mistake. The mountain at that place was about a mile high, and almost perpendicular. The face of the mountain was covered with sharp loose rocks. Up this I climbed a distance of half a mile, to a rocky bench, above which towered a perpendicular bluff of immense height. Here no horses could climb, and I lay down in a crevice for several hours, famished with hunger. I had had nothing to eat since the night before, when I had eaten the piece of salmon. I pulled up as much grass as I could find, to keep me from the damp ground. In the afternoon, when the sun got round the mountain, it grew so cold I could not stay there. I had no materials for a fire, and should not have dared use them if I had. The bluff above me was as near perpendicular as nature ever formed rough rocks. I determined to get on top of the bluff. I started, and got up about thirty feet, and found then that every rock I took hold of was loose. I looked about me to see how to get back, and the scene was frightful.

The little bench I had left was not to be seen, and it appeared, if I fell, that I should go down ten or twelve hundred feet over craggy precipices, into the Columbia. I had to lay my head back on my shoulders to see above me. I can hardly describe the terrors of my situation, or the painful labors by which I surmounted them. After working about an hour and a half, I managed to reach the top, completely exhausted. Getting on a knoll, where the sunbeams made a little warmth, I laid down and fell asleep. It was so cold I only slept about twenty minutes, and then wandered about for Indian roots to appease my gnawing hunger. I saw a springy place a few rods from the top of the mountain, and there found some roots, which tasted to me better than any food I had ever eaten. I then went down to the Columbia by another route, and traveled up the river about eight miles, till about nine o'clock that night. I was then so exhausted I could travel no more, and crept into a patch of large weeds, breaking and bending them over me, so as to leave no trace of my presence. I lay there and studied on my situation for some four hours, and finally dropped asleep. When I woke up I was nicely covered with snow. I could see it was daylight, but I neither knew nor cared what time it was. Some hours after I awoke I heard voices. I carefully raised the weeds, and looked to see who it was. There were about five Indians, a hundred yards distant, coming towards me. Being covered by the snow, all signs of me were obliterated. When they came near, I heard one of them say, "If we catch him again he will not get away from us." I judged they meant to kill me at once. I lay still, and they rode so close to me that they shook the weeds over me. I stayed about two hours, when they returned, passing by to their camp.

It was still snowing. After they had passed, I got up and went on up the river. I had nothing to eat, and had no chance to get anything, except from the Indians. I scratched in the snow, and got the tops of some wild mustard, which is much stronger than cultivated mustard. This I ate. I commonly wear number eight shoes, but my feet at this time were so swollen that I don't think there was ever made a pair of shoes large enough to hold them. I traveled about fifteen miles. Then, at the distance of about four hundred yards ahead of me, I saw a small command of government troops coming down towards me. I thought for a moment whether to give myself up, and be exposed to the world, or to wander along and take my chances of starving to death. I concluded to walk off the road and lie down, and see if they would notice anything. If not, I would take my chances. While they were approaching me, I looked back on the ridge about three miles, and saw the Indians coming. Knowing that the Indians would track and find me in the snow, I preferred to give myself up to white men. When the command had all passed but one man, I rose up and told him that I wanted to get on behind him, and go back with him. I was so poor, from starvation, that this man did not recognize me, although I had been with him for months before. I got on behind him, told him who I was, and rode up to the officer, and he ordered a horse for me. I rode without a saddle about twenty-three miles, to John Day's river. I still lived, but that was all. I was raw all over—poor as a snake; my wounds, especially the one in my thigh, still giving excruciating pains. But I made no complaints. I informed the officer that I had a saddle there, and two pairs of blankets, and my pistols, which had all been recovered. The saddle and blankets he got for me. By the aid of these I rode more comfortably. The Indians told the officer he could ford the river about a mile above.

The Indians who had captured me before had sent word to

Jackson that they had taken me, and that I had escaped. Knowing I was somewhere in that region, Jackson came out with a body of men and met us at the fording place. I shook hands with him. I rode up to him, but was so much changed by suffering that he did not recognize me until I spoke to him. He treated me to a drink of liquor. He had with him five white men and some thirty mounted armed Indians, to capture one starved and worn-out sinner. The Indians were much enraged at my late escape from them, and the large reward that vanished with me. We camped for the night about a mile and a half below on the river. I had nothing to eat yet but a small piece of bread that one of the soldiers gave me, and greedily devoured a good meal that I got that night. The soldiers were all friends of mine, and would have favored my escape, had there been opportunity. About dark it commenced raining and snowing. I lay down on my blankets, and the sheriff of that county, who was with Jackson, put a pair of hand-cuffs on me. Jackson told me that his credit had about run out since he had lost his *capital* (meaning his prisoner). He laughed and talked, and seemed much rejoiced that he had me again. He relished the joke more than I did.

About nine o'clock the sheriff of the county came to me and said he would take a portion of the responsibility on himself, and fastened a hand-cuff round one of my wrists, and the other cuff round his. He fastened himself to a virtual corpse, for I was so weak I could scarcely move. Next morning the hand-cuffs were taken off, and we started for Fort Dalles. When we started, the Indians joined us to go to the Fort to get their recompense for looking me up; and I was escorted by a band of about one hundred and fifty men. We rode very fast through the snow and rain, some forty-five miles, and arrived at the Fort about three o'clock in the afternoon, on the 3d of March, 1857. I had been gone on the pleasure excursion I described, just thirty-one days, and during that time had suffered over and over far more than death could inflict upon me. I had not had a warm meal of victuals; most of the time without sufficient clothing; had never allowed myself a fire; wandering about over the snow and sharp rocks without shoes, with wounds of a frightful character; necessitated to keep my faculties always on the alert to avoid the Indians, and at the end of this experience was reduced to a mere skeleton. Nothing but an unconquerable will, and an equal tenacity of life, could have kept my soul in my body. If physical and mental suffering can atone for a mis-step in life, I fully atoned for mine. When I look back at that period, it seems like a frightful dream.

At the Fort, Jackson went to the commander for a place to put a prisoner. A cell in the guard-house was assigned to me. There was I put, with my wet blankets, on the ground, after riding all day in the rain. About nine o'clock that night the little drummer boy brought me some cold bread and meat.

This was the only time that Jackson neglected me. He went down in town to rejoice over my capture, and got drunk. He was so much addicted to liquor that he went by the name of "Whisky Jackson." He did not forget, however, to have me securely ironed. A bar of iron about a foot long, with my wrists fastened at each end, was put on to me, securely riveted. This apparatus was put on so tightly that my wrists swelled. The next day, the military officer, seeing the pain I was in, took me to the blacksmith's shop, and had the clavices on my wrists enlarged. A shackle was riveted on each leg, with a large chain connecting them, about two feet long. In the middle of that chain was a heavy trace chain, about ten feet long. This dragged on the ground and only loaded me down. The shirt that I had worn from the time I was placed in my bed after being wounded, I wore all the way to Downieville, without change. I lay there till the fourth day, when Jackson, the Sheriff of the County, and myself, started by steamboat for Portland.

The first day we got to the Cascades and lay on the boat that night. Next morning I was removed to a hotel. After dinner we went in a wagon six miles to the Lower Cascades. The road being very bad, we were too long on the trip to reach the Lower Cascades in time for the steamboat. We went to a hotel and waited there two nights for the boat. On the second day we reached Portland. The boat lay out in the stream, and they did not allow me to go on shore. My friends had raised five hundred dollars for my lawyer, and I was to pay him five hundred dollars more. Jackson had no requisition from the Governor of California or authority from the Governor of Oregon, and there was also a flaw in the warrant. My lawyer came on the boat but did not speak to me. He told some of my friends that he would do nothing while I was on the boat, but if I was brought on shore he would get me out of the hands of the authorities. The Sheriff, learning these facts, was much perplexed. On the next morning he and Jackson talked of returning to Fort Vancouver and putting me in the guard-house. But they did not carry out this real or pretended intention. Finding a schooner in the Columbia river, under command of Capt. Beatty, I was transported from the steamboat to the schooner. The Sheriff insisted upon the Captain bringing me to California, but he would not do it, and said I could stay there until a boat passed for Astoria, at the mouth of the Columbia.

The schooner was loading with flour, potatoes, &c., for California. The schooner dropped down about ten miles that day, and Jackson expressed himself much pleased to think he had outwitted my friends and lawyer, who did not know where I was, but would suppose I had gone in the steamer for Fort Vancouver. At that place the schooner finished its load. Next day the steamer bound for Astoria came along, and I was put on board of it. On going down in the steamboat, S. Blair, on board, was found out to be the captain of the *J. R. Whiting*, a schooner at Astoria, about to start for San Francisco. Beatty had said he would not take me for $500. Blair, who was a jovial, good-natured

LUMBER SHIPS TAKING ON THEIR CARGO.

fellow, said he was going, and if we saw fit to go on his boat, he would give us the best he had. At Astoria, I was transported to his schooner, which was loaded mostly with lumber. It was a 175 ton schooner. The deck was filled three feet above the rail with lumber, except just at the cabin. Capt. Blair was very attentive to me, and spent much of his time talking to me after my transportation to his boat.

On the third day we started out, the Oregon Sheriff there leaving us. I was not much sea sick. I was still more emaciated than when I was retaken, and extremely weak.

[*At this moment several little girls came and looked into the grated window where we were writing. The prisoner requested them to leave and come in the afternoon when we would not be so busy; and then turning to me he said: "I can never speak kind enough to those little things—they seem to be so innocent and pure."—S.*]

Jackson was somewhat sea sick. He had been so much in the habit of drinking, that when he happened to be without liquor—the captain keeping none on his boat—he became very light headed, and needed some stimulant to keep him up. We both kept our bed most of the time for three days. I would occasionally get up and walk on the lumber, to bid the shores of Oregon "good-bye." I could yet see the blue mountains in the distance. After the third day I was on deck most of the time. The cook often invited me to come into the cook room to get warm; but Jackson would not let me.

When about twenty miles out from the Heads it was very

rough—the schooner pitching and rolling heavily. The captain said we were going about six miles an hour. We were in sight of the light house. Jackson was pacing from one end of the boat to the other, on the lumber, and climbing into the rigging, and had the captain's large spy glass in his hand. He remarked to me: "It would not surprise me, if I fell overboard." He had made a staggering step several times. At the time, I was sitting on the top of the cabin about four feet from the man at the wheel, right in front of the man, his face towards me. The captain was about three feet from the man at the wheel, taking the sun, I think. Jackson was walking on the lumber. The last I saw of him he was about twelve feet from me, standing on the edge of the boat, with the spy glass raised, looking through it at the light house. The man at the wheel afterwards swore to the captain that Jackson was twelve feet from me, and that I was sitting on the cabin. The lumber was piled above the top of the cabin. I heard an exclamation and a splash in the water. I raised up and grabbed my chain. The captain at the moment whirled round, and threw off a lot of lumber, and at the same moment shouted: "A man overboard!"

Jackson, at the time, was swimming about twelve feet from the boat. He did not speak. On the cook hearing the cry of the captain, he rushed out of the cabin and threw over the life stool to within a few feet of him. Jackson was still close to the boat. All hands were on the lumber in a moment, and a small boat unfastened and lowered in about ten minutes—Jackson still in sight, and swimming. The waves tossed the lumber and life stool so that he could not get hold of any of the things thrown to him. When the boat was launched, four men jumped into it, and put out for him. The wheel was left, and every man did everything he could for Jackson's rescue.

There were eight men on board, besides Jackson and myself. I was on the cabin, and the Captain asked me where he was. I shewed him. Jackson was almost three hundred yards behind—the tide running furiously out of the Heads. The men in the boat got within sight of him, say within sixty or seventy yards, when he sunk. So the mate said when they returned. The boat could make little progress in such a sea. The Captain remarked, "Jackson was a good swimmer; he kept up in those waves full twenty minutes." I think he must have floated at least fifteen minutes. While the boat was gone, the Captain turned to me, and said "Did you push him over?" I said "No, sir." Said he, "I am afraid you did." Said I, "ask the man at the wheel." The man at the wheel had gone in the boat. When he returned, the Captain called up all hands. The man at the wheel said I did not do it. He shewed the Captain where Jackson was standing, in a tottering manner on the edge of the boat, using the spy-glass, and that he seemed not to be aware he was so near the edge of the boat, but seemed to put one foot forward, and found nothing to put it on till it reached the water. He also shewed him where I was sitting at the time, on the cabin, twelve feet from Jackson, full in his own sight. The Captain turned to me and said "I don't believe you did do it." All the hands on the boat seemed to be satisfied that I did not do it.

About two hours after this occurrence, I went into the cabin and got some grease, greased my hands, and slipped off my shackles, and threw them overboard. The Captain told me I ought not to have done that, and asked me why I did it. I told

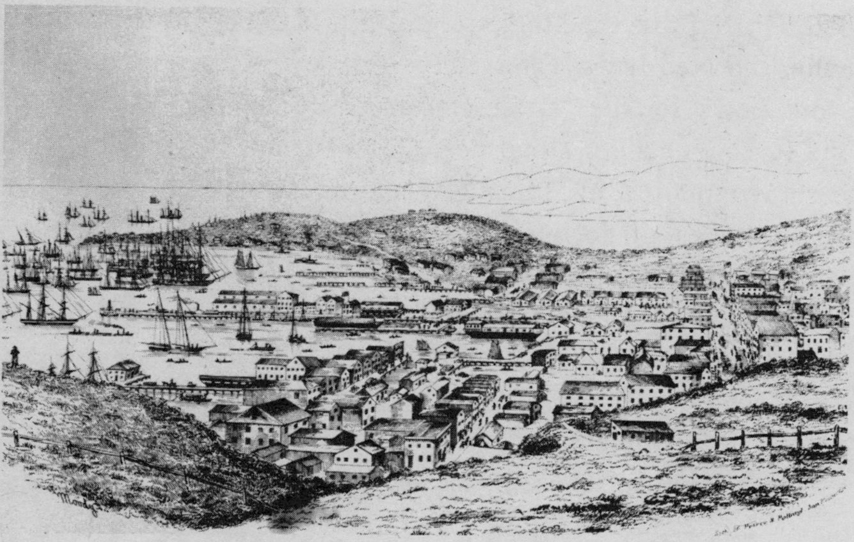

San Francisco, from Telegraph Hill.

him I had worn them until my wrists were sore, and I had come to the conclusion not to wear them when I could pull them off. He told me he would have to tie my hands. I told him I was willing. The mate wrapped some cloths around my wrists, and put on a cord in such a manner that I could have taken it off any moment. The Captain was nearly distracted at Jackson falling overboard. He said he would not have had it happen for all the vessel and load. The day after, we got into San Francisco, about night. I stayed in the cabin until the Captain went ashore and brought officers. In making his return of his boat, as he told me, he put in that he had a prisoner on board, and that the Sheriff who was bringing me down fell overboard. I appeal to Capt. Blair and his men, for the strict truth of this statement. I was taken to the station house by the officers, and the second day to jail. During this time they telegraphed to the officers at Downieville, and Ned Irwin, Sheriff, and Frank Proctor, Under Sheriff, came down for me. These officers treated me kindly, and took me to Downieville. I had been absent from Downieville about eighteen months, and during that time had passed through adventures enough for an ordinary life-time.

I have said that my real name is M. C. Bolin. To the public I have for several years been known as David Butler. I changed my name in 1853, at the time I was drawn into gambling. I had been with a man by that name, and got it fixed to me as a nickname from that circumstance. The first time I saw it written, a friend of mine put it on the books of the Beatty Hotel, Grass

NEVADA CITY.

Valley. I had been called by the name the night before, at Rough & Ready. I never denied my real name, and often told it afterwards. At Forest City, I told it to John Kirkpatrick, to T. A. Reed, and to F. Winters, and others, well known gentlemen there. I allowed myself to be called Butler, to keep my real name from disgrace, and that my friends at home might not hear of it as worn by a gambler. At Forest City, I joined the American party, and then gave my real name. At Downieville, after being brought back, my counsel, hearing that Butler was not my real name, asked me if it was. I told him that it was not, but that I preferred to go by that name, so that if I was sent to the State Prison, I might afterwards return home, and still keep the shame and disgrace from my people. I told him that if I got clear, I would explain everything, and never use the Butler name again.

It is not necessary for me to trace my history from this point, as it is well known to the public. I desire, however, to express my thanks to S. Clapp, the Jailor at Downieville, and his excellent wife, for the kind treatment they afforded me in my imprisonment at that place. They treated a poor, broken down outcast, as a man and a brother, and my last thoughts will be full of affection for them.

I have thus given to the public a faithful account of my life. They can judge in how far I am criminal, and how far persecuted. I have been abused and pressed on account of Jackon's death. When arguments failed in regard to Moffat, it was urged that I at any rate murdered Jackson, and if hung, it was all right on general principles. This has been the tone of some of the press, since my conviction, as well as before. In regard to that, Jackson took the chances of capturing me. If I was the cause of his death, it was only by being the cause of his trip. He unfortunately fell overboard, but it was not my act, and out of my power to prevent. I had nothing to gain by his death, no mountains to fly to, no facilities for escape. The character in which I was on board the boat was known to every one on it; and his death, so far from favoring my escape, must diminish the chances for it. He was careless in his watch over me, as is proved in my previous escape from him. I had good reason to think that he would get drunk on getting to San Francisco, and that I could slip off while he was after officers, or forgot to get them, in passing a whisky-shop. But when the responsibility of keeping me should be transferred to the Captain, I had no chance to elude him. Had the idea ever entered my head of pushing Jackson from the deck, I was not such an idiot as not to weigh such objections to the act. Besides, I was not a murderer in heart. I had not intended to kill Moffat, and I certainly would not peril my soul by killing one not more a man than Jackson.

I have always felt that I did not deserve the fate to which I am hastening. But I have long since ceased to struggle against it. My example may be a warning to others, of the consequences of the lesser vices, and how far a man may be betrayed in an unwary hour into a position from which his soul would naturally revolt. After I was lodged in jail, I sought and availed myself of no means of escape, except those afforded by the law. I may confidently appeal to the officers who have had me in charge, if my conduct has not been correct in every respect, since I was lodged in jail. I have aimed for, and believe I have possessed their esteem. With energies restored, and life stretching far beyond me, were it not so soon to be cut ignominiously off, were there room for hope, I might desire an opportunity to redeem my good name. But hope is dead, and I can but address myself to the future. This troubled dream will soon be over, and I trust to rest in peace.

EPILOGUE

Being an Account of the Execution of Major C. Bolin, from the Nevada (*City*) Democrat, *March 3, 1858*

M. C. Bolin, *alias* David Butler, who was tried and convicted in this county of the murder of Robert Moffat, at Downieville, in September 1855, was executed last Friday. He was tried under the name of Butler, and by that name only has he been known until a few days ago, when his true name was made public, there being no further inducement for him to conceal it. Bolin, in accordance with his own request, was brought out of jail at twelve o'clock, and got into a carriage which was in readiness at the door. In the same carriage were Reverends Dryden and Warren, and the jailors, Messrs. Lenhart and McFadden. The Nevada Rifles under command of Lieut. Phil. Moore, formed around the carriage and kept the crowd at a respectful distance. Sheriff Boring, Deputy Van Hagan, and Ex-Sheriff Butterfield, of Nevada, and Sheriff Irwin and Deputy Proctor of Sierra, followed immediately behind the carriage on horseback. The gallows had been erected on the other side of Lost Hill, about half a mile from the Court House. An immense crowd started for the gallows with the carriage, the most of them going ahead. On arriving at the place of execution, the rifle company cleared the ground immediately around the gallows, the officers and a few others remaining inside the circle. The doomed man then got out of the carriage, walked to the gallows without assistance and run briskly up the steps. He was dressed in black. The officers of Nevada and Sierra counties, the two clergymen, and Mr. Sargent, his attorney, went upon the scaffold. Mr. Boring then read the death warrant, also the respite of Gov. Johnson. Bolin then turning his face toward the crowd on the west, spoke nearly as follows:

"I have this to say to the dying friends I leave behind; that you will give up the follies of this world, and be prepared to die. I would to God I could live always, for the benefit of my friends. I see many friends here. It comes my time now to die. I trust in God, and soon expect to be in His presence. I hope this example will be a warning to you all. My advice is to you all, to shun bad company, ever be your own counsel, and never be led astray by the bad. I feel for you all. You no doubt feel for me. I much regret that I must die and leave my friends behind; but we must all die and leave friends, and you will soon follow me. I don't think I have had justice done me, but I am soon going to where I expect to get justice. I have had my life published for the benefit of those I leave behind. I have read it over since it was printed. It is the statement I made, mostly in my own language, and is true. I wish you could see your folly as I see mine. There are many around me indulging in the same bad habits which has brought me to this end—thousands around me. My parents were kind to me—well advised me as a child, but I have not heeded their advice. I leave sisters and a brother behind. I trust God will protect them."

Bolin then turned his face in an opposite direction, and repeated the substance of the remarks given above. He spoke in a subdued, solemn tone, but with a firm voice. Some fifteen or twenty of his acquaintances then came forward and shook hands with him and he bid them all a last good bye. Then holding up the pamphlet containing the narrative of his life, he said:

"This is the statement I have made; it is a true one. You will probably many of you read it; when you do so, I wish you to regard it as the statement of a dying man. My conscience is clear of murder. I now return thanks to the officers who have had charge of me. They have treated me as a brother. We are all born to die. God gave our lives, and he can take them. I have been a great sinner, but I feel that I have made my peace with God. I wish I could live to advise those with whom I have heretofore associated; but I cannot, and if my death will be any warning to them, I am reconciled to die. The sting of death don't seem to be any horror on my mind. Death is preferable to being thus exposed to the world to the disgrace of my people. I have been in prison thirteen months—in chains. I have been visited by many ladies and children. They all spoke kindly to me, and many of the children wept. They reminded me of my childhood days. It seems but a few days since I was a child at home. I strayed from home, was led into bad company, and have been a great sinner. I trust to meet you all in a happier land. If I could think of another word that would benefit you, I would speak it. I much regret to give up this life, but a man does not fear to die when he is prepared. I trust we shall again meet in a land where we will part no more.

"I will say a final farewell to all—a final farewell to all. I hope my fate will be a warning to all. Let those who admire the follies of this world take warning.

Let worldly minds the world pursue,
    It hath no charms for me.
Once I admired its follies too,
    But God hath set me free.
Farewell to all, forever."

He then shook hands with those on the scaffold, pulled off his boots, took his handkerchief from his pocket and threw it over among the crowd. His arms and feet were pinioned, and after taking a last look at the world, the black cap was drawn over his face. He then requested of Mr. Boring that his body should be buried in the same clothes he then wore and that a letter which he had received from a friend should be left in his pocket. The rope was then adjusted by the two sheriffs, a prayer was made by Rev. Mr. Dryden, and at the word "amen," the rope was cut by Mr. Boring, the drop fell, and at 1:40 p.m. the body of Bolin was suspended in the air. He made one or two slight struggles, and all was over. Twenty minutes after, Dr. Bailey announced that

A California hanging in the 1850's.

life was extinct. The body hung about thirty minutes, and was then cut down and placed in a coffin and given to his friends.

Bolin stood on the scaffold a little over an hour, and bore up to the very last with the most heroic firmness. There was nothing of the bravado in his words or actions; he seemed to fully realize his situation; did not conceal his regret at leaving the world, but exhibited no craven fear of death.

As the crowd returned into town they were counted, and numbered 4,516. Quite a number left for their homes without coming back, and probably not less than 5,000 people witnessed the execution; among whom were about twenty women.

Index

COLOPHON

The *NARRATIVE OF THE ADVENTURES OF MAJOR C. BOLON, ALIAS DAVID BUTLER AS RELATED BY HIMSELF TO A.A. SARGENT,* was printed in the workshop of Glen Adams, which is located in the quiet country village of Fairfield, southeast Spokane County in Washington state and one township removed from the Idaho line. Fairfield is located on state highway 27 that runs between Opportunity and Tekoa. There was an early newspaper account printed about the death of Major C. Bolin, and in 1966 the late Lewis Osborne then of Palo Alto, California, published a tastefully done version of the life and adventures of Major Bolin. This Ye Galleon printing uses the typesetting of Lewis Osborne, to whom I give my thanks. Mr. Osborne later moved to Ashland, Oregon where I became acquainted with him by telephone conversation. Camera/darkroom work for this edition was by Susan Paulson, who designed a fresh title page, yet one using the original Osborne typesetting. Susan Paulson also photographed the existing pages and made the printing plates. Additional typesetting was by Teresa Ruggles. The sheets were run by Vernon Stevens on a Heidelberg press model KORS. The paper stock is 50 pound tan offset. Folding was by Garry Adams using a 26 x 40 Baum Dial-O-Matic folding machine. Assembly of the folded signatures was by Garry Adams. Hard case binding was by Al and Melissa Chidester of Oakesdale, Washington. This was a fun project. We had no special difficulty with the work. This is the 580th book to come from Ye Galleon Press.

The travels of Major C. Bolin while he was a fugitive, and after his capture by deputy-sheriff "Whisky" Jackson, are indicated by the red lines on this map.

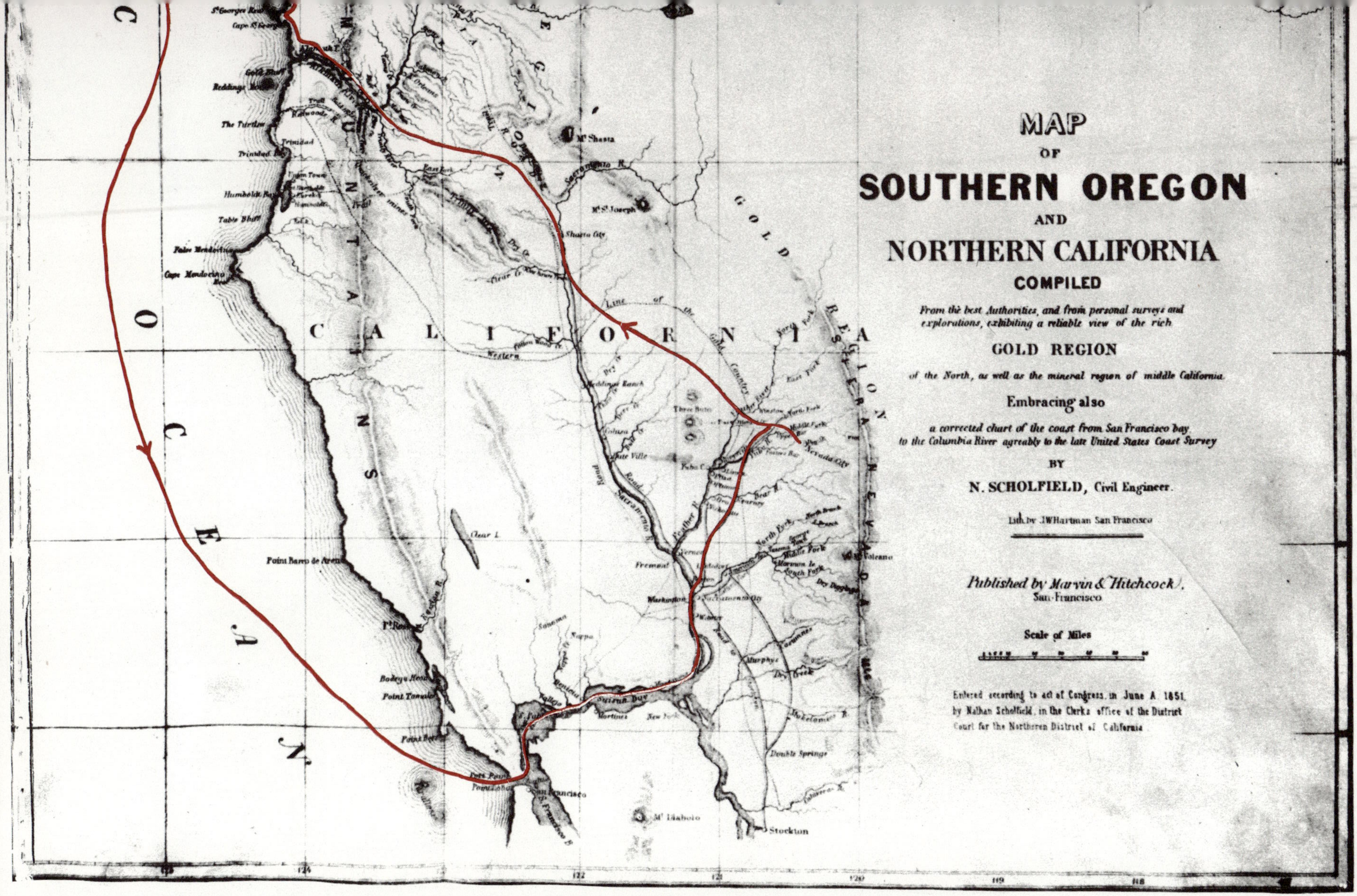
MAP
OF
SOUTHERN OREGON
AND
NORTHERN CALIFORNIA
COMPILED
From the best Authorities, and from personal surveys and explorations, exhibiting a reliable view of the rich
GOLD REGION
of the North, as well as the mineral region of middle California
Embracing also
a corrected chart of the coast from San Francisco bay to the Columbia River agreably to the late United States Coast Survey
BY
N. SCHOLFIELD, Civil Engineer.
Lith. by J.W.Hartman San Francisco
Published by Marvin & Hitchcock,
San-Francisco
Scale of Miles
Entered according to act of Congress, in June A. 1851, by Nathan Scholfield, in the Clerks office of the District Court for the Northern District of California
GOLD REGION
SIERRA NEVADA
CALIFORNIA
OCEAN
Mt. Shasta
Mt. St. Joseph
Shasta City
Humboldt Bay
Table Bluff
Cape Mendocino
Trinidad
Point Baro de Arena
Bodega Head
Point Tomales
Sonoma
Suisun Bay
Sacramento R.
Feather R.
Sacramento City
Fremont
Washington
Nevada City
Stockton
San Francisco
Mt. Diabolo
Double Springs
Murphys
Clear L.
Redding Ranch
Colusa
Three Butte
St. Georges Reef
Cape St. George